A Ten Million $ Testament

A Ten Million $ Testament

Revised

Pia Pikwah Fields

A Ten Million $ Testament — Revised
Copyright © 2025 by Pia Pikwah Fields

All rights reserved. No part of this publication may be reproduced, distributed, or transmitted in any form or by any means, including photocopying, recording, or other electronic or mechanical methods, without the prior written permission of the publisher or author, except in the case of brief quotations embodied in critical reviews and certain other noncommercial uses permitted by copyright law.

Although every precaution has been taken to verify the accuracy of the information contained herein, the author and publisher assume no responsibility for any errors or omissions. No liability is assumed for damages that may result from the use of information contained within.

Library of Congress Control Number: XXXXXXX
Paperback: 979-8-9930791-4-1

Printed in the United States of America

Contents

Chapter 1:	After Sydney's third wife died	1
Chapter 2:	Sydney's Childhood	8
Chapter 3:	Sydney's First Marriage	18
Chapter 4:	Sydney and His Second Wife	26
Chapter 5:	Richard's Marriage	43
Chapter 6:	Sydney's Testament and a "Probate Will"	73
Chapter 7:	Challenge the Probate Will	84
Charter 8:	Forgery, Perjury Undue Influence and Duress	105
Chapter 9:	Deposition	115
Chapter 10:	Obtain Strong Evident	136
Chapter 11:	Court Hearing and Judge's decision	142
Chapter 12:	Appeal	151
Chapter 13:	Proposal for decreasing government's debt	167
Chapter 14:	Postscript	178

Chapter 1
AFTER SYDNEY'S THIRD WIFE DIED

The sound of a bell in a church is getting louder and louder when the camera moves from the sky to a hall room where there is a funeral: flowers surround a woman's picture. Under it says "Teresa Fishman (1932–2014)." The pictures and flowers fill the screen.

A ninety-six-year-old blind man, Sydney Fields, is sitting in a sofa and listening the guests introducing themselves one by one. Sydney knocks his head to them. He looks relieved with no upset.

Camera focuses on an old lady, the words in the screen list Rosa Palmer, Teresa's sister.

Rosa

Syd, you have to take care of yourself now. I am very upset for the situation, my sister **passed** away. *Remember*, you are still my family member. We will always take care of you and make sure you are comfortable at home.

Camera focuses on a woman in her fifties. She looks educated greedy.

Diana

Uncle Syd, you take care. Teresa is my aunt but treated me as her daughter all her life. I tried hard to arrange this funeral and hope it is okay for you.

Camera focuses on a man in his fifties.

Victor

Uncle Syd, I am Victor, Teresa's nephew, I just came back from Hawaii yesterday. I am sorry that I never stayed around you since I finished college. I appreciated that you made Teresa gave me all the money she inherits from you. Even though we didn't see each other for decades, you know that I love my aunt and you. My aunt loved me, as well. I feel sorry that she left so early, hope you take care.

Camera focuses on a woman with two children.

Cinthia

Uncle Syd, I am Sandi, niece of Teresa. Hope you take care of yourself well when such a sad thing happened. I am sorry that every time I come up New York City from South Carolina, I didn't have time to see you because my son is autistic who always screams and cries. However, not seeing you doesn't mean that I do not miss you.

Camera focuses on the last woman in her fifties.

Ana

Uncle Syd, I am Ana Maria Garzon Yepez, daughter of Teresa's brother. Even though I never met you until this year, my aunt mentioned about you for many times. In my mind, you are my family member. I live in Ecuador all my life.

Sydney

I know all of you. It is good that we have chance to meet each other today. You all take care. I will be OK.

Ext

Around a table in the corner of the mourning hall.

The four women and one man sitting together and stay away from Sydney

Diana

It is too bad! Our aunt was twelve years younger but died before him. She told me many times that the inheritance she had from Syd will be sure go to our family. Eight years ago, I tried very hard to make her understood that as a wife, she has right to share at least 50 percent of Sydney's asset even though he is alive. It could be even more after he passed away.

Victor

What do you mean? Uncle Syd once told me that all his asset was made by him alone before they got marry. Our aunt worked for a church all her life as a bookkeeper. Before retired her annual salary was only thirty thousand dollars and she had left all her savings to us. Particular now, aunt has already died, she had no children with Sydney. He can take everything back. We are done.

Diana

It is truth that his first will reflected his real intention. It said after our aunt passing away 60 percent of the inheritance, she had from him must go back to his grandchildren, 40 percent go to charity. That means he just let our aunt kept the fund while she alive and she has no right to manage any of them. That is why I spent a lot of time to tell our aunt about her right as his wife. She finally made him set up his second will and allow our aunt could actually arrange 50% of his asset. Our aunt will give all those money to us because she considered we are her children

Victor

I knew what you did in those days. Sydney was blind and he had to rely on our aunt. He had no choice but he was very angry. He complained to me on phone and said you unduly influenced our aunt. He made clear in the second will that the 50 percent inherits Terisa aunt took from him must all straight forward to me. You get nothing and you can't challenge his decision. No one can probate his will except our aunt.

Diana

I know what he means in his second will, for punishing me he forced aunt left everything to you. Unfortunately, our aunt died now and that means you will get nothing as well. You have no choice but cooperate with us. Aunt told me that his assets are worth ten million dollars. Want it or not, up to you.

Cinthia

Yes, the situation has changed entirely. We all agreed that we must do something and we all deserve something.

Ana

Including me. You can't ignore me because I know your plan.

A legend showing:

A ten-million-dollar testament

Ext In an apartment, 19th floor of a building near Central Park

Sydney is talking on phone with Jeffry kern, a broker from Vanguard.

Sydney

Good morning, Mr. Jeffry Kern. This is Sydney Fishman. My wife died one week ago. I want to transfer all the money back to my individual accounts. I did that in Chase Bank already. All I need is show them her death certificate. You know that those money actually are my money. I added her name in my account because she is twelve years younger than me. I thought I would die before her.

Jeffry

I am sorry to hear that. Of course, you can arrange your funds. For transferring your fund, you need to fill out some forms. I have mailed that to you, did you receive it?

Sydney

Yes, I have them. But I didn't do anything because I can't read. You know, I'm legally blind, although I—that's not like being actually blind, but I can't read. I can't read, I can't read any typed words, you know, and that's why I can't handle those papers. I can't fill out those, those papers that were mailed to me.

Jeffry

Can you see them at all to read them, or even if you—?

Sydney

I-I-I-I can't. I can't read them, no, I can't read. I mean, with my magnifying glass, I can read large print, but I can't read anything that's—that's on, that's on papers.

Jeffry

Okay

Sydney

I was wondering if I could go to your office and like I did in Chase Bank. I, sat in front of a girl, answered her questions and the fund transferring was done.

Jeffry

We are in Philadelphia. You are ninety-six-year-old and blind, we can't let you travel a few hours from New York to make the transferring. Do you believe that your attorney could be able to help you to fill out with this form? We can finish the transfers on phone? Do you

Sydney

No, no. No, I am no, no, he has—he doesn't know anything about these forms. I am not discussing any forms with him.

Jeffry

Okay. My group here was asking if there was somebody that you trust to read the forms to you, and we could do a conference call to answer any question.

Sydney

Well, I, I mean, I have a niece that, that's that helps me read a letter sometimes. I mean, she, knows nothing, nothing about, about, about, about the law or anything. I don't know whether she can interpret the forms. I, I haven't, I haven't, I haven't, I haven't shown any of the forms to her. I-I thought, I thought you were going to make arrangements there to see me about the forms. I don't mind to travel.

Ext.

Jeffry

I understand. I will make a trip to help you.

Sydney

You mean you will come to my apartment to see me. That is too good. Thank you, Thank you very much.

Ext.

Jeffry, a man in his thirties, rings the doorbell. A lady opens the door; she is Ana, the niece of Teresa.

Ana

Please come in. Mr. Sydney Fishman is waiting for you.

Process for transferring funds

Jeffry talks to his coworker on the phone. After they let Sydney state his password, staffs from Vanguard read the account number and then read the fund amounts that need to be transferred: Three million dollars transfer to account #235406... Two million dollars transfer 2354061 ... two million dollars transfer to 2354049...

Jeffry

Mr. Fishman, according to your request, your funds in Vanguard, $7,865,800, are all under your name except the account that was mentioned in your wife's will. As your indication, that is her savings, and you are not going to touch them. Right?

Sydney

Correct. Thank you very much that you came over to New York and solve a big problem for me. I am planning travel to Philadelphia. I accumulate these monies all my life only for my family, two sons, and three grandchildren. Unfortunately, for some reason, I didn't see them in the last twenty years. I think of them every day. I suffered a lot and hope can live as longer as I could. It is not easy for a blind man. My wife is twelve years younger than me. If I died before her, she will keep 50% of my asset. Now I have everything back and I can leave all of them to my children. I finally have a chance to proof how much I love them. You know I have no father. My father passed away one day before I was born. I know how sad a family without a father is for a family. I tried hard to be a good father and continue the family line. I work six days a week till late night, and my only wish is to bring my family to a middle class ... I suffered a lot for that, and my children suffer a lot, as well.

Movie goes back to one hundred years ago.

Chapter 2

SYDNEY'S CHILDHOOD

Ext. In a farm house in New York upstate. The young man is sick in bed. A doctor and pregnant lady are around him.

Voice

In 1919, the Spanish flu was spread all over the world and killed 26 million people. `Samuel Fishman emigrated from Russia to the United States for just a few years.

He caught the Spanish flu before the New Year eve of 1919.

The camera pushes to the doctor, who at his twenties, was working at Samuel's home.

Introduction show on the screen: Dr. Philip H. Groginsky from NYU medical school is identified.

Doctor stares at the patient seriously. Next to him is a pregnant woman in her twenties. She is crying and shaking Samuel's body.

Bessy

Samuel, wake up, please. You can't leave me alone like that. We have a baby coming and our son Rick is autistic. I need help! I need help!

Doctor Groginsky

You should stay away from here for the baby in your stomach and for your child here.

(The doctor turns toward a child sitting at the corner of the room. He is quite and looks restart)

I will try my best to save your husband. Your job at this moment is to calm down and take care of yourself. You are the backbone of this family now

Bessy

(Bessy screaming)

No, no! If he goes, I will go with him!

Samuel

Sorry, I have to leave now, but I will never abandon you. I will never ...

Ext. Samuel's spirit flies up to the heavens, passes through a very black tunnel. Over there, he meets an angel.

Samuel

May I go back into that body? They need me.

Angel

No. It is too late. But you can get back there as a newborn baby. You will not have a father and have to struggle alone all your life.

Samuel

Struggle is okay, but do I have a successful life that allows me to make big money?

Angel

If you want big fortune, you have to suffer a lot, as well as your family members. If you just get rational money, you will have a good family relationship, nice wife, and wise children.

Samuel

But will my family eventually own and enjoy the money I earn since they suffer for that? Shouldn't they deserve something good as well?

Angel

I know what you mean. You have to try first. The situation will be complicated. You have to fight a lot and suffer a lot in your life as well as your family member. You can't control anything. It also depends on if people willing to give you their hands, particular a girl, your future daughter in-law.

Samuel

Okay, for my son and my family. I will try.

Samuel's spirit jumps to the earth…

Ext. Back to the farmhouse. Bessy screams and grasping Samuel's dead body when it is moving out of their home. The doctor looks helpless and tries to stops her. Bessy makes another extreme scream again, holding her stomach. Blood is come down along her leg. The doctor moves Bessy to the bed and takes care of her.

Doctor Groginsky

Your baby is due two months earlier. Push him out hard please.

Camara shows a pot of hot water and sound make by scissors is hearing, and then a baby's crying.

Doctor Groginsky

You have a boy! You have another boy now. He is small because due in seven months, but is healthy. You must be strong! You are the only one who can help Fishman family continue their line now.

The doctor wipes his tears when he's talking to the mother. He signs a death certificate and then a birth certificate. He bites his finger and leaves a bloody fingerprint on the birth certificate to witness the baby's birth.

Voice

Doctor Groginsky watch tragedy happened in Fishermen's home and risked his life to help them. He doesn't know that his behavior touches a lady seventy years after. In 1988, the new born baby's son Richard Fishman meet Pia in New York Hunter College and told her his family stories. Pia pictures how a woman watching her husband's dead body was moved out and giving a baby born. She also admires the doctor's brave and even worry for his safety. Driven by the unselfish doctor's behavior she agrees to marry Richard and carries the fourth generation for the family.

Pia doesn't realize that Richard was kind of autistic and doesn't know how to deal with people. Because of that he creates more tragedies for the family. In 2008, one hundred years after Sydney was born, Pia spent one hundred thousand dollars on legal fees to protect Sydney's ten-million-dollar assets. Knowing how Fishman's family members suffered Pia can't stand the five relative's in-law of Sydney's third wife steal all Sydney's money and left his family nothing. She believes if God gave the family a hand one hundred years ago, God should not let it sink today. She not just appeals she publish the case into a book and write a script.

The tragedy related to Sydney Fishman was continued.

Ext. A table with two little girls and two little boys, Sydney and Rick. There are a few dishes on the table. Children are staring at the food. Bessy divides the food into two parts. She leaves one part on the table and speaks to the girls.

Bessy

Girls you will eat with your father together. OK?

Bessy takes Sydney and his retard brother aside. She divides the food in two bowls, gives one to the brother and gives the other bowl to Sydney. When Sydney finishes his share, he cries and wants more. Bessy is holding him tightly and holding back her tears as well.

Ext. A man in his thirties open the door and walks in. Bessy goes toward him and take the bag in his hand.

Bessy

Denny, is everything good today? Dinner is ready. I let Sydney and his brother eat first because they are hungry. I made your two daughters wait for you. They are nice girls.

Denny holding Bessy's hand and spoke

Bessy, thanks you take care of my daughters. Their mother was so sad when she died for Spanish flu. Our girls were only three years old and five years old.

Bessy

As a mother, I understand her feeling. We are lucky to have you as well. You work so hard to support us financially.

Denny

Two families were united together, that is the only way we can do in these difficult days. *(He holds Bessy face and look at her seriously)* Let us go ahead together. I love you Bessy!

Denny puts food in his children's bowl and puts some in Bessy's bowl. He looks tired but feels satisfied when watches the kids eating.

Ext. In a construction field. Denny is carrying something heavy. He falls onto the floor all of a sudden. Workers near him rush to take a look. **Denny** laying on the floor and spoke

I hope can see my wife. If no time, please tell her I love her and I am sorry. He then stopped breathing Denny's co-workers sit with Bessy and comfort her.

One Worker

He told me he didn't have enough food. He was hungry, weak, or maybe sick, as well. He said he love you and he was sorry;

Bessy

Oh, he never told me he was hungry. He left his food to us, and he died because of us. (Bessy cries aloud.)

Ext. Bessy and three kids sitting in front of a grave with the name of Denny Kumman. Sad expression shown on her face. Her second husband died ten years after her first husband died. They were dead at about the same month and same day. Bessy is confused and cries to the sky.

Bessy

Why it happens again and again.... No more marriage ... no more marriage ... It's enough, it's enough. Why do you treat me like that? God, why do you treat me like that?

Voice of Angel

According to the commitment, some tragedy must happen. As what we told Samul, for being rich, all Sydney's family members must be suffer and have miserable lives. It is destiny that they can't avoid.

Ext. Bessy, the two girls, and Rick.

Bessy

Elizabet and Rose, I have to go out to work to make money now. I can't take care of you anymore. You have to stay with your grandmother like before. God bless you. Rick and Sydney, you will stay in your grandpa's home. You will have your uncles as company. I will bring food home after I finishing work.

Ext. At night. Bessy goes home with a few potatoes in her hands. She splits those potatoes into two parts, giving Sydney one and Rick the other one.

Sydney finishes his share immediately, and Rick holds the potatoes carefully, looks at them, and eats a little bit. Sydney watches his brother eating and wants more. He yelling and crying. Rick hands his share to Sydney, and has tears in his eyes.

Ext. In the apartment Bessy work. She is a housekeeper there.

She says goodbye to her master who hand some food to her

Master

Give this to your children.

Bessy

Thank you. I will see you tomorrow.

Ext in a riverbank near Bessy's home. Bessy sees a group of people around there. Her brother, David, is surrounded, and on the floor is a child's body. Bessy screams and jump toward them. That is her son Rick.

David is weeping.

Bessy

What happened? I told you to watch him carefully! How come you let him fall into the river?

When I was playing basketball, he ran toward the deep water. He never acted like that before. I don't know why. I can't watch him every minute. He is seven years old. He should know outside of the river is dangers ...

Bessy

(She cries and yells.)

My poor baby, why did you do that! Why did you do that? Why? Why?

Ext. In grandpa's home. Sydney was sitting alone and eating. He looks at the place where his brother Rick usually sat, he breaks out and crying loudly.

Ext. in the back yard of grandpa's home Sydney jumps up to the back seat of his uncle's bicycle. David is ten years older than him.

Sydney

Let's go, Uncle David, I am ready.

They go to a forest with a wide area of grass. They play baseball with other youths. After a while, Sydney sitting on the shoulders of Uncle David and then stands up slowly for climbing up to a tree. David then climbs up to the tree, as well. They sit together and watch far away as the sunlight mixes with fog. The landscape is beautiful. It represents an unknown future for these youths. David then jumps down to the ground. Sydney dares not do it.

David

Jump, don't be afraid. I am here to catch you. If you do it, I will give you some of my lunch. I know you always hope can have more to eat.

Sydney jumps down, and David didn't catch him, but Sydney is OK.

David

You know you can make it. You must be confident first. They then sit down together, and David keeps his promise, gives half of his bread to Sydney.

Sydney

Uncle David, you are so nice to me. I feel secure and powerful when stay with you. You know I have no father; I am self-abasement in front of the other kids. I am lucky to have you.

David

You see, you will always have me. I catch you, as I promised.

You grow up now. You know we must be aggressive and bolt, do something that people dare not to do. That is why I told you to jump down from that tree. It is a challenge.

Ext. Bessy is cleaning a bathroom, as a housekeeper.

Ext. Sydney's grandfather Louis selling things in the street to make a living. The movie screen shows the words "1928 to 1930, economic recession."

Ext. Sydney's two uncles, twenty-two years old and seventeen years old, are walking along the street, from one store to another one, asking if there are jobs available. When they get home it was dark. They look frustrated and tired.

Ext. Again they walk on the street, try to land a job, and again go home without hope.

Ext. In Grandpa's home Uncle David doesn't get up one morning. He has killed himself with gas and has left a note.

Voice

"Sorry, there is no job for me no matter how hard I tried. I don't want to be the burden of my family, and dying is my best choice. Let me go to the world that belongs to me."

Ext. Sydney is sitting on the same tree that David told him to jump. He is crying and yelling loudly alone. He gazes at the sky where clouds are moving and spreading around. A lightning is exposing in the sky. David's uncles' faces appear back and forth in Sydney's face. He feels extremely lonely. He is crying loudly while the rain is pouring down.

Sydney

David, Uncle, why do you leave me alone like that? You know I have no father. I consider you are my father. Brave to kill yourself. Is that what you mean by bolt?

Sydney keeps crying and jumps to the ground. His face is facing down and lost his consciousness.

Ext. One years later, in the same room.

Sydney's other uncle kills himself with a gun. A note is shown in the scenery.

Voice

"I don't have a job. If this world doesn't have a place for me, why should I insist to stay alive? I choose to follow my brother with dignity rather than beg for a job. I am sorry Sydney, if you want to continue, you go ahead"

Voice

Sydney's four family members, his step father, his brother and his two uncles all die in his childhood. God lets him encounter the most horrible experience. He has to pay for being rich.

Chapter 3

SYDNEY'S FIRST MARRIAGE

Ext. The entrance of a college gate shows the City College of New York. Sydney is walking out from there. He then goes to a supermarket, works as a stock boy, and puts things on the store shelves. He then sits down and does the accounting work. He takes care of everything in the supermarket. A young girl is sitting next to him. She is the daughter of the boss in the supermarket.

The boss, James, calls the girl.

James

Alice, go home for dinner. You can help with nothing here.

Alice

No. I want to stay with Sydney till he finishes working then go home.

James

(*He sighs and hand him some money*)

Sydney, you can go home now. Continue tomorrow after finishing school.

Ext. Sydney goes home and gives his salary to his mother.

Sydney

Mother, you quit that servant job and cook for me at home. My salary is enough to take care of the family.

Bessy

My poor baby, you are just seventeen years old. You don't have a father. (*She cries again.*)

Sydney

I know, mama. You suffered a lot, as well, I'm grown-up now, and let me take care of you.

Ext. Sydney and James are talking in the office.

James

Syd, you are old enough to get married. My daughter, Alice, loves you very much. If you don't mind, I hope you marry her. You take care of her, and I will take care of you as your father. I will have a house as your marriage gift. At least you can settle down.

Sydney

Thank you, my dad.

Ext. In a church Sydney and Alice wear wedding clothes on their wedding day. They pass rings to each other. Then they face each other to express their vows of love.

Sydney

I take you, to be my wife, to have and to hold from this day forward. For better or for worse, for richer or for poorer, in sickness and in health, I promise to love and cherish you.

Alice jumps up, holding Sydney's neck and hang her on him

Sydney carrying the little Alice in his arms and walking out of the church. A satisfied feeling is on his face, as if he were a general who just won a battle.

One year later . . .

Ext. In a basement, Alice is giving birth to their baby. She is screaming, and a newborn baby is crying. Sydney is delighted when he finds out he has a boy. He is holding Alice's hand and carries the baby meanwhile.

Sydney

Sweetheart, thank you. We have a son. Our son.

Alice

Leave me alone.

(She turns away with cool, sad expression on her face, tears are falling. She is gazing her baby and doesn't look excited about being a mother.)

Ext. Alice sitting in the living room and holding the baby. Sydney going home from outside.

Sydney

Sweetheart, how are you today? How is the baby?

He gets no answer.

Sydney

What is for dinner?

Alice

I didn't make anything. You just cook whatever you like.

Ext. Sydney is holding a piece of bread and drinking a bottle of wine.

Sydney

Sweetheart, I hope we can be together tonight. Can you take a shower before that? You have not taken a shower for almost a month. It is not good to be holding our child when you smell bad.

Alice

Leave me alone. I am taking care of him, and he will be fine.

Sydney is approaching his son and wants to carry him. Alice screams. Sydney is very helpless, confused, and upset.

Ext. Sydney sits with James, Alice's father.

Sydney

Three years have passed already. If it's just baby blues, she should be getting better, but nothing was improved. Our baby is three years old now. He needs a normal and healthy growing environment, not dealing with a mother who is stinking and silent. She does not allow us to take our baby away from her for even one minute.

James

I am sorry. I didn't expect things to happen like that. I see you already have a lot of patients. As her husband, you have the right to make a decision. Maybe we can give her a little bit more time.

Sydney

You know, I had no sex with her for three years. She is yielding when I touch her. I can't live like that for the rest of my life. Our child Kenny has no normal love from his mother. Now he is three years old and needs to learn things from outside environments and deal with other children. She treats him like a prisoner but hardly talk with him. I am going to let a psychiatrist test her. If they believe she should go to the hospital, I will have a court order to send her there. Me and my son's future can't be tied up with her in this way.

Ext. A psychiatrist is in the basement of Sydney and Alice's home. Alice is screaming and running around. Her hair is long and dirty; her clothes are dirty and messy.

Ext. In a courtroom, there is Sydney, Alice, a policeman, and the psychiatrist.

Judge

Do you have a medical report for this case? Does Sydney Fishman want to send his wife Alice Fishman to a mental hospital?

Sydney

Let us hear psychiatrist, Mr. Robinson Neil's opinion?

Neil

I am a psychiatrist for twenty years. Alice's problem is more serious than baby blues. Someone with baby blues usually recovers a few months after the baby is born. It has been three years already. She hardly talks with people, nor to her parents and husband. She refuses to take a shower, does not cook, and does not go for shopping. She screams when people approach her child. She treats her son like a prisoner. It will be not good for a child who grows up in this kind of environment.

Judge

What is your suggestion?

Neil

Our medical center has the place to settle these kinds of patients. She belongs there. She is not qualified to take care of her son.

Judge

Husband Sydney, do you agree with that proposal?

Sydney

I have nothing against it.

Alice

I screamed because I always have a dream that they will take my child away and shut me down behind bars. I feel so helpless when they're approaching me. Nobody backs me up, not even my parents. *(She cries again.)*

Judge

Your feeling is right. Nobody can help you, not even me, not even the law. Now only God can bless you.

Ext. At a mental hospital, Alice is behind bars. She still looks dirty and sad. Sydney is holding a card and hands it to her.

Sydney

Our son, Kenny, is five years old now. He could write his name. This is a card he sent to you. It says it is for his mother.

Alice

Why don't you take him here and let me see him? I miss him every minute, but I can never see him since I was put here. I prefer to die if I can't see him.

Sydney

I am sorry. You will not see him again. I can't let my son know he has a crazy mother like you. I have to consider the psychological effect on him.

Alice

(She is crying.)

You took my son, you shut me up, and you did not keep the promise in the marriage vows: you will take care of me when I am sick. Not only that, you torture me by taking my son away.

Sydney

You did not commit to your vows in the marriage neither. You did not take responsibility as a wife and a mother. The court allowed me to have an annulment with you because of that. My lawyer will send you the annulment judgment. By the way, I have sold our house. As your committer, I have the right to do it. I will use the money to raise our son, Kenny, and send him to a good school.

I promise the money I get from your house will all go to him.

Alice

You took my son, sold my house, and put me behind bars. (*Alice cries loudly.*)

Sydney walks away and leaves Alice behind. Tears fill in his eyes. When he gets out of the mental hospital, he sits on a bench in a park; he then kneels on the ground and gazing the sky.

Voice

This is one of the tortures your family member has to take for you being rich. Remember we have a commitment.

Sydney

(*Yelling to the sky, seems like he hears the voice.*)

It is so ugly! If I know it is so cruel and sad, I will not deal with you. My hand is dirty now. My hand is dirty now. (He looks at his hands.) Alice, I promise you, all the money I have from your house and all the money I make in the future will go to our son.

Ext. Sydney's son, Kenny, grows up in his mother's family with James and James's wife.

Ext. Kenny stays with his grandmother Bessy. Running around without a home, he is a miserable child.

Voice of the Angle

Sydney's wife has to suffer, as well as his son. Again, this is a commitment that almost nobody knows. Sydney made it with us before he was born, and he doesn't even realize that now.

Chapter 4

SYDNEY AND HIS SECOND WIFE

Ext. Beach—day.

Sydney is at the beach alone. He is looking around and sees a lady not far from him is reading a book, on a beach chair. The lady, Gladys, turns to him, as well.

Sydney

Hi. Are you being alone here?

Gladys

Yes, I am a schoolteacher and having a summer vacation now. I am from New York City.

Sydney

It just so happens I am from New York City too. I am an accountant. They sit closer and continue talking.

Ext. At a New York restaurant, Sydney and Gladys are on a date.

Sydney

It is nice to know you. It has been three months already.

Gladys

Nice to meet you too. My sister is younger than me but got married thirteen years ago. I am thirty-five years old, and I am still waiting for the right person.

Sydney

Can I be your Mr. Right? I got married for one time, and I have a son. I'm divorced because my son's mother is in a mental hospital.

Gladsys

I don't mind that you got married before. I just hope you have only me from now on.

Sydney

Will you take care of my son, Kenny, as well?

Gladys

Yes, I will. I will work, submit my salary to my family, and do all the housework. I can be a perfect wife.

Ext. On a stormy night, a wedding party is held at a restaurant. Guests are walking in with bad mood.

Voice

Sydney's second wedding takes place in the biggest storm of the century. It looks like even God not bless them from the beginning. Sydney's marriage turns out to be a big mess again.

Ext. In an apartment of New York City, downtown Manhattan. There is Sydney's new home for his second marriage. He is talking with his clients from his accounting business. He invited them for dinner because he has his own home and a new wife now. His clients watch the clock again and again. Sydney knows what that means.

Sydney

I am sorry. My wife is a school teacher. We just got married, and I don't know that she is not good at cooking. Dinner was supposed to start at seven o'clock, and now it is eight thirty. Let me find out what happened.

Ext. A table is ready, with a few sandwiches and a chicken boiled in water. The chicken meat is white and bland and has no sauce.

Gladys

Food is ready. I am sorry. This is what I cooked, sandwich and chicken cooked in water.

Sydney's guests look at one another and say nothing.

Ext. Sydney and Gladys are on their bed and get ready to sleep.

Sydney

I didn't know that you don't know cook at all. You never learned?

Gladys

I did learn, but I still just know how to put things on the bread or put things into water. My mother said I am terrible at cooking. Maybe she is right.

Sydney

Looks like I can never entertain my guests or friends at home.

Gladys

You better don't. Professional women usually don't know how to cook, but they can carry a baby.

Ext. In an apartment Sydney is holding a newborn baby.

Sydney

I kept my promise to give you a child. His name will be Richard Jack Fishman. "Jack" is for the memory of you father. I know it is not easy to have a baby for a woman at her forty-three years old. I will try my best to keep the marriage even though we are not getting along that well. We got married after we'd known each other for only three months. I hope we had known each other more.

Gladys

Don't you see I am trying my best? I do all the housework, and I give you all my salary. There is not a woman who will handle things like that. I don't mind doing it because you are my husband. I want to please you. We are happy when we are together. You are a CP A, a good career in people's minds. That is all I care about. We have to maintain the marriage to the end, no matter what. I will never divorce.

Sydney

If you keep your promise, including take care of Kenny, I will not divorce for the sake of our son, Richard. But you should have your own social life with your friends, such as your coworkers or the students' parents. You cannot hold all your hopes in our marriage.

Gladys

I don't deal with them, my coworkers, or students' parents. They are all from low class. I told them my husband is a CPA. They don't like to hear that. Lt looks like they can't wait to see me get a divorce and laugh at my face.

Sydney

Oh my god, you really don't know how to socialize. You can't condemn people like that. I am not as rich as you think, and I am not that good. You know that our marriage has problems.

Gladys

(She is screaming.)

How can you say we have problems? We have no problems! We are match for each other. If you come back for dinner in time, I will have nothing to complain.

Sydney

You are too dominating. Even though you don't complain, I complain. I can't invite clients to have dinner at home. I have to go to a res- taurant for keeping good relationships with them.

Ext. Kenny going home at night. He sees all his stuff, his books, his clothes, and his baseball bat, are in the hallway. He is crying there.

Gladys

You don't come home for dinner. I spend two hours to cook, and you hang out with friends and don't even bother to call me. It's enough for me. I am not going to take care of you. You go! Go back to your grandmother's home.

Kenny

Right, I don't have a home. You are not my mother. You curse or yell all the time. It makes me scared. I prefer to hang out late when I have friends as company.

Ext. Sydney gets home at that moment and hears their arguments. Kenny runs to his father and cries even more loudly.

Kenny

Father, I don't have a home. You promised to give me a home, but I don't have it. She is crazy. I am scared every minute when she is around.

Sydney

Alright, alright. She has a bad temper, not just for you. She doesn't treat her own son nice neither. I will get rid of her. I promise my children will be the most important members in my life. Trust me that I will get rid of her because of the things she did today.

Sydney no longer sleeps with Gladys since that day. He goes on vacation once in a while without taking Gladys with him.

Ext. Sydney coming with a suitcase. He takes out his keys and opens the door. The door is not open. His neighbor passes by.

Neighbor

I saw a locksmith work here yesterday. Maybe he changed a broken lock.

Didn't your wife tell you?

Sydney

Thank you. She might not know I came back from trip today.

Ext. Sydney is packing his stuff. Gladys is mad and throws things on the floor. She is using scissors to cut Sydney's shirts. Sydney grabs them back.

Sydney

I think we cannot continue like that anymore. You are hyper, panicky, and turn out to be hysterical. You fight with my child Kenny for no reason. You changed locks twice when I was away. Since you don't want me to come back, I move. You and Richard can continue living here, this apartment with three bedrooms and facing the river. You just need to pay a few hundred dollars rent every month and the government will pay the rest. You should be fine to handle it with the income as a teacher. I will pay you child support meanwhile. Hope you have good luck.

Gladys

You're a bitch. You want to divorce. You wish! I am your wife. We were together for eight years, and you can't get rid of me like you get rid of a piece of garbage. People will be laugh at my face everywhere. My sister, my mother, my coworkers. I prefer to die if you make me divorce you. I will get you! I will get you!

Sydney slams the door and goes. Gladys continues to throw all the things in the apartment. She has totally lost her mind.

Ext. In a hallway. Gladys is moving with Richard, her four-year-old son. She giving up that apartment Syd left her

Richard

Mom, where are we going? Why give up our home?

Gladys

This is not our home anymore because your father will not come back. I have rented an apartment in the building where he is living now. You go kick his door for me.

Ext. Richard is kicking the door, and neighbors are going out to look. Sydney opens the door and grabs his son into the apartment.

Sydney

Richard, you are my son. I will never abandon you. I just cannot stand your mother anymore. I will go out with you every Sunday. That is the only day I am off, and I give all my time to you. Okay?

Richard

I am scared when you are not around. Mom cries and yells constantly. I don't want to go home.

Sydney holds his son, and tears are in his eyes.

Sydney

I am sorry. Be a good boy. She will not hurt you. You just ignore what she said.

Ext. Richard stands behind a fence in a playground and watches children play. He wants to join them but is grabbed back by his grandmother and grandaunt.

Voice from the Movie

Richard is a quiet boy. He, just like his mother, doesn't know how to socialize. His mother, grandmother and grandaunt surround him. They consider him a kid who always needs to be protected and not allow him play with other children.

Grandmother

They are low class. You are a multi millionaire's son. Let us go home.

Ext. Richard puts water in the bathtub and drowns his cats in it. He watches them struggle in the water and die.

Grandmother

What are you doing? You feed them every day. You don't have affection for them?

Richard

I don't know what you mean. You said I should know how the other people or animals feel? I can't tell that. People are not nice to me. I will not be nice to them either.

Ext. Richard is in school. He wears glasses at his age of six. His clothes were bought from thrift stores by his mother. Children always laugh at his face and take his glasses away. He runs after them. They pass his glasses from one kid to another.

Ext. One day, Richard sees the kid who harassing him frequently passing through a door. He bangs the door in front of his face and hits the kid hard. When see the kid is sent to the hospital by ambulance Richard has a winner's look on his face.

Ext. Gladys is in the office of the school president.

School President

Your son can't stay in this school any more. We can't keep him.

Ext. Gladys takes Richard from school to school, asking for enrollment. They also have to move from one apartment to another apartment for the new school.

Ext. In Halway,on trucks,Gladysmoving again and again when Richard was kicked out of the school again and again Richard has a cold hateful expression on his face.

Gladys

You are driving me crazy! We move every year. I am still paying the rent for the previous apartment because I had a lease with the landlord. Now we have to move again.

Richard

It is not my fault. They harass me first. They insult me. I have to teach them a lesson. That is what my father told me.

Ext. Sydney and Richard are in Central Park. Richard is riding a bicycle.

Sydney

Let's go. Quick.

Richard tries to catch his father and loses his balance. He falls to the floor.

Ext Richard and Sydney are on a big rock slope of Central Park, eight feet from the ground.

Sydney

Jump. Be a brave kid and jump down. I will catch you.

Richard looks around and is scared. He finally jumps, and Sydney doesn't catch him. Uncle David's face is flashing in his mind.

Ext. In a hospital Richard get hurt when he jumps down to the ground from the rock slope.

Sydney

Doctor, why don't you make more stiches? Is that enough?

Doctor

If you so care about your son, why did you tell a kid to jump from such a high place?

Sydney

This is the way Jews train their kids. I just followed what they said.

Ext. Richard is home. Gladys is checking her son's wound. Ext. In Glady's apartment

Gladys

Your father wants to kill you. I am telling you seriously, you should not listen to him. You should not go out with him anymore. You must stand on my side all the time. He wants to throw us away. He wants to divorce me. (Gladys starts to cry again.)

Ext. In a lawyer's office. Sydney is talking to a lawyer.

Sydney

I am going to divorce my son's mother Gladys. We have been married eight years but actually stayed together for only five years, then separated. She wants to take big money from me, but all the money I made had nothing to do with her. Can you give any suggestion to me for keeping my asset?

Lawyer

US laws usually protect women. You know that, particularly since she has a son with you. The judge might give her 50 percent of your asset. Divorce in Mexico can avoid judge's decision here. If you can make her sign a paper there, you can file it here, Americans still recognize Mexican divorce today.

Sydney

Can you take care of it for me? I pay you and her airplane ticket and rent you motel rooms at the border of Mexico. She was dumped. She is desperate for money. I will give her $110 a week in the agreement and let her sign a paper. We don't have to tell her what the paper is. She will sign it, for her salary is just $600 a month.

Ext. At the lobby of a Mexican motel. Gladys's and Sydney's lawyers are sitting together. The lawyer takes out a paper from his bag. Gladys signs it without even looking.

Gladys

Here it is. You said I will have $110 a week if I sign it, right? America only recognizes the divorce process inside US. I don't think the paper signed in here is recognized by our government.

Lawyer

Thank you. Mrs. Fishman. I will guarantee that you will have your money.

Ext. Sydney is playing chess with Richard.

Sydney

Teacher said you are very good at playing chess. You will have the New York City middle school tournament next week.

Richard

Daddy, I know I will win. My IQ is over 154. I just got a test. I am a genius I don't like to deal with people. I should be a lawyer; my mother told me.

Sydney

You can't survive in the real world if you don't know how to deal with people. You must know how people think about your behaviors. If they like it? If you hurt them? Don't act like your mother? She has a bad temper, and she doesn't care about other people's feelings. She just wants what she wants. I have divorced her already. I am sorry we can't sit down together to arrange your problem. You have talent at playing chess, but it is not easy to make a living by doing that.

Ext. At a chess tournament, the chess club is giving out a reward to Richard Fishman. Sydney is sitting down at the audience's seat. He is happy and clapping his hand. When Richard goes down from the terrace, Sydney shakes people's hands.

Sydney

I am Richard's father. I am the one taught him chess but don't have time to play with him. I don't know he can play so well.

The referee

He is a genius. I just check his IQ; it is over 150. You should encourage him develop in this field.

Voice

Sydney knows that Richard can't socialize with people. He doesn't know how to raise questions to maintain conversations and make friends. He doesn't know and never care how the other people think. He can answer basic questions but can't maintain relationships with anybody. Sydney doesn't realize that Richard's slowness at socializing is actually a symptom of autism that make him a genius in some field. His parents' negligence ruins Richard's whole life. He was considered schizophrenia eventually.

Ext. Richard is walking out of his apartment building, and he is angry. Sydney is driving a car to follow him.

Sydney

Do you know that your mother will be thrown out of her apartment at the end of this month? She can't pay rent. She lost her job, and you will be a homeless soon.

Richard

I know. It is because you divorced her. She cries whole day long. She doesn't go to work. She was fired. You created this trouble for us.

Sydney

I am done with her. She should stand on her own feet. Many women can handle their lives well after divorce. You know her temper. I can't be tied up with her all my life. I will take care of you if you lost your apartment. Don't blame your father. Okay?

Ext. It is winter, windy and snowing. Gladys is walking in Manhattan, from the Ninth Street to One-Hundredth Street. She walks step by step, heavily like an angry soldier in marching. She is crying meanwhile

Ext. Richard is sitting alone in front of a table, eating food his mother put there, like a cat eating things the master puts down. Richard looks at the clock, it is nine o'clock at night.

Ext. Gladys and Richard drag two suitcases at the Forty-Second Street train station of Manhattan. Richard carries his trophy from the chess tournament.

Gladys

You should call your father. I will go to the shelter. I can't let my son live on there. I will let people know how a multimillionaire forced his wife to live in a shelter.

Ext. in front of Richard's school Sydney shows up to pick up Richard. Glady is there as well

Sydney

I will take care of Richard. I talked to the president in your school and contacted the education department of New York City. They said, since you've worked more than twenty years in school, you can simply retire. They will give you the pension and give everything they own you. You can just apply for the retirement and accept their decision, not file a case to challenge them. The paper you signed in Mexico is a legal divorce paper. You wasted your money to fight. I see you double- endorse all the child-support checks I pay you and gave to the lawyer. You threw money to the fire.

Gladys

You get out of my face. I will find a lawyer, fight against you. You will never have a peaceful life.

Ext. In a small apartment in Manhattan, Sydney is helping Richard arrange his stuff. It is a small but bright apartment at the top of the building.

Sydney

I paid big money to have a lease for this apartment. It is close to Hunter College, and you can register there. I also have a job for you, at a clothes store, Bolton, right in the corner. I will pay for your rent, will see you every week, and take you out for dinner. You have to work in the store for your pocket money.

Ext. Richard is carrying a box at the store and raise it high to the shell. He put hands in his forehead and said I have fever.

Ext. Richard is having dinner with his father at restaurant. Ext. Richard sees his mother at a park.

Gladys

Your father should send you to law school, not to a city college. Your father is the boss of Bolton. I saw him sitting with Bolton's boss. How can he let you be a stock boy and make you work when you are sick?

Ext. Richard is sleep in his apartment. Sydney walks in. He keeps shaking Richard. Richard opens his eyes.

Sydney

I thought you'd never wake up. The super told me there is gas leaking in this building. I rush here. The gas leaking has stopped. I hope you didn't get hurt.

Richard

I am okay now. No wonder I smelled something wrong and I fell asleep.

Ext. Richard and Gladys sitting at the park.

Gladys

Your father is an evil. He wants to kill you. He is the one who made the gas leak. You should move there as soon as possible. I have my lawyer get the money back from the education department of NYC. We will have thirty thousand dollars in savings now plus two thousand pension a month. I can rent an apartment for us now. I will give you four hundred dollars allowance a month.

Richard

Father said you don't need a lawyer to take the money back. City has their rule: they will surely give you money that belongs to you. How much have you paid the lawyer?

Gladys

The lawyer kept 50 percent of what I got. It is about thirty thousand dollars. They said they can help me overthrow the divorce. I only need to give them five hundred dollars a month as legal fee. It is all your father's fault. He is supposed to send you to law school, but now he wants to kill you.

Voice

Gladys runs her life to the hell. She takes Sydney to court. She gives all her money to the lawyers to make a hopeless fight. During those days, she becomes more and more crazy. She is cursing Sydney every ten minutes and drives Richard crazy. Richard has become angry and restless. He writes a lot of letters to attack his father.

Letter 1: "You are not a good father. All my high school classmates are happy to mention what good school they are going to enroll. I have nothing to say because I don't have my father to discuss my future with me. I can only go to City College even though I have good grades."

Letter 2: As the son of a multimillionaire boss of Bolton, I had to move boxes up and down in a store even I was sick.

Letter 3. "You made gas leak in my apartment, and you want to kill me."

Voice of angle

The fates of Sydney's second wife and second child are sad, as well. They are driven crazy little by little. The tortures they endure are not less terrible than the first wife has. Again, this is the commitment Sydney made with us for the ten million he will have. He even doesn't realize the connection between all the troubles he had in his life.

Chapter 5

RICHARD'S MARRIAGE

Ext. In a classroom for summer course. Richard sits on the first line. He is upset, never talks to people, but always answers the professor's question instantly and correctly. Behind him is a Chinese lady who looks like she is at her late twenties, but she is actually thirty-eight years old. She wears fashionable earrings and has nice smile on her face. Her name is Pia. One day, Richard approaches her.

Richard

Hi. My name is Richard Fishman. Can we study together for the test?

Pia

Fine. We can invite that girl, Amy, together with us.

Richard

No problem.

Ext. In Central Park. Pia and Richard are sitting on the grass.

Pia

Why did Amy not come?

Richard

Oh. I told her the study is canceled.

Pia

How can you handle things like that?

Richard

Because I want to stay with you alone.

Pia

The economics course we have is stupid. Its theories believe that they can control the whole economy by simply playing with the interest rates. They encourage consumption but makes the society become a throw-away society. They believe an unseen hand, supply and demand, can run the whole society by creating jobs. To make economics fields become scientific, they need a fixed formula to explain humans' activities. They believe the supply and demand is what they want.

Richard

I only memorized what they said. Only in that way I can have a good grade. My index is 4. Hi. Can we be friends? I mean be girlfriend and boyfriend.

Pia

How old are you? I am thirty-seven years old already. I think I am much older than you.

Richard

I am twenty-five years old. I don't mind the difference of age. Men can be older than women. Why can't women be older than men? Why do we use double standards?

Pia

You don't care, but your parents might care.

Richard

They have nothing to do with my business. My father's not seeing me anymore. My mother is crazy. She cries and curses every day. She lost her mind because she was abandoned by my father. I need my own home. I want to stay away from them.

Ext. Richard is holding Pia's hand tightly. They walk to YMCA, where Richard and his mother live temporarily.

Ext. inside a YMCA room, Richard grabs a ring from a drawer and puts it on Pia's hand. That ring does not fit. It has capital R on it.

Richard

I don't have time to prepare anything. This is the ring I found on the street. Please allow me to use that as an engagement ring.

Pia does not have happy feeling for that. She is in contemplation, didn't say yes or no. Ext. Day 1, Richard insists to send Pia back to her home in Queens.

Ext. Day 2, they hang out on the street after finishing school.

Ext. Day 3, they hang out on the street till late, and Richard insists to send Pia back to Queens.

Ext. Day 4. They hang out on the street and holding hands. Gladys meets them accidentally and yells at Richard.

Gladys

What happened here?

Richard

Mom. This is Pia, a girl I just knew and I will marry her.

Gladys

You are a rich man's son. You cannot marry whoever you meet in the street.

Richard

She is my classmate. We get along well. You control all my life. You can't continue do it. I will have my own life now.

Gladys

(She turns to Pia.)

This is my family business. You can go home now. I don't like you seeing each other. No way.

Richard

(Talking to his mother)

I want to let you know that if it's between you and her, I will choose her, not you.

Gladys

She is not white. She is older than you. What do you need her for?

Richard

Age, skin color is not what I consider. You and my father both are white Jews and your ages are close. See how your relationship is.

Gladys's bad attitude doesn't affect Pia. In her eyes, Richard's determination shows that he is a person who has his own ideas and really knows what he is doing. Pia is touched that a man chose her rather than his mother. She feels that she cannot say no to a man like that.

Ext. Pia and Richard are in front of a building lobby in Manhattan.

Richard

Could you tell Sydney Fishman, who lives in 20P, that his son hopes to see him?

Doorman (after making a phone call) He says no.

Ext. Richard and Pia are at Central Park. Richard is crying loudly.

Richard

You see now, my mother is crazy, and my father ignores me. My father was born one day after his father died. The same doctor signed the death certificate and birth certificate for the family. That was during the 1918 Spanish flu, which killed twenty-six million people. Maybe that is why he was cruel. He always said, "I don't have a father. You should struggle like you don't have a father as well"

Pia

You mean a doctor risked his life to help your family? Your grandmother watching her husband's dead body carried out when she gave birth to your father? What a picture, a brave doctor and a despair mother!

Pia's mind is distracted by the scenery.

Richard

Yes, my grandmother Bessy was very unhappy all her life. She only smiles when seeing me. I was three years old then. My mother always took me to the hospital to visit her. She loved me very much, but now, nobody cares about me.

(Richard cries loudly again.)

Pia has never seen a man crying like that. She comforts Richard.

Pia

Don't worry. I will take care of you. Like the brave doctor, do something for your family, a poor family.

Richard

That means you agree to marry me?

Richard is delighted, like a child with a big smile.

Richard

When will we register? I can't wait for even one day. I have a suit for a wedding.

Pia

Maybe Wednesday.

Pia can't say no at that moment after Richard is just crying sadly.

Ext. In front of the college entrance Richard is waiting. He wears a suit (before, he always wore a vest) and has a big smile on his face. Pia walks toward Richard. She looks at Richard seriously.

Pia

Registering marriage needs money. Do you have money with you?

A young man who always wears a vest that seems to not have a pocket to put money in. She hopes he forgot to take money and she can reject him for that reason.

Richard

Yes. I have money!

Richard shows a big smile again. He feels the chance is even closer. He looks like a child. Pia says nothing. She just feels that she can't play a game with Richard, who looks so eager like a child.

Pia

Okay. Let us go! Let us not worry about the future! Any problem should have a way to solve it

Ext. At the park outside the city hall, for the wedding day. Pia wears a white dress left by her sister in the closet and puts a crown of flowers on her head. She and Richard have a wedding picture before that.

Voice from the Movie

Pia doesn't know so many problems are waiting her to solve.

Pia has been waiting for the right man all her life. She never expected her wedding coming like that: no excitement, no expectation, no happy feeling. It's just like getting into an adventure, curious to see what will happen.

Ext. Pia and Richard in an apartment.

Pia

I registered for our marriage without telling my parent. It's luck that my sister agreed to be our witness when we swore in front of the judge. We get married now, as you wish. This is our home. You put down the ten thousand dollars your mother gave you and my sister gave us as mortgage loan to own this apartment. Living next to my family, we can get help easily.

Richard

I appreciate that. Sweetheart, I will work very hard and study very hard for you. Tomorrow I will have my job, work in a reception position, answer phone for a company. They accepted me right away.

Ext. In front of an office reception desk, Richard keeps dialing the phone. A few policemen walk in.

Policeman

Hi. We need to see your boss. Someone in this office keeps dialing a number to tight up an office. They call 911, and that is why we are here.

A man, office manager, comes out from an office room and looks at Richard.

Manager

I am the manager here. Must be this boy who did it. Nobody in this office has time to keep dialing phone numbers, except him. He is new here. I will get rid of him.

Policeman

The other side said if those calls are stopped, we don't need to arrest anybody.

Manager

(asking Richard)

Why did you do that? You can go home now. We don't need a crazy troublemaker.

Ext. At their new home, Richard talks to Pia.

Richard

I got fired. Sitting in front of a telephone, I can't help to dial numbers related to my father's clients. When their phone keeps ringing, they will know it is me and will tell my father about that. That is one of the ways I catch my father's attention. I need him to always think of me.

Pia

Oh my god! You don't have consideration. How can you catch your father's attention by harassing his clients on phone? Make him mad, giving you no benefits? I have listened to you and put our marriage news in the New York Times. Your father must have noticed that already.

Ext. Richard hits Pia all of a sudden and then holds her to cry.

Richard

Actually, I married you is just for causing my father's attention. He refused to talk to me since I ran away from the apartment, he rented for me. Now I got marriage he still gives no response. It drives me crazy and I feel like I might explode anytime and make violence actions. He keeps contact with his uncle Sol. We can visit him in California and he will contact my father.

Ext. At a California airport, Pia and Richard are waiting. They seem worried.

Richard

How about if Uncle Sol doesn't show up? I hardly contact him in my life. I don't know how he thinks about me. He might think I am crazy and refuse to see me.

Pia

We are already here. Let us see. If he does not shows up, we can rent a motel room. It is first time you take an airplane. Just for that, this trip is worth.

A seventy-year-old man walks straight to Pia and Richard and stretches out his hands to them.

Sol

This is Sol. I know you are Richard, for next to you must be Pia. Welcome!

Sol turns to Pia.

Pia

We appreciate your coming to pick us up. I do worry that you are mad at Richard, just like his father is, and will refuse to see us.

Sol

You traveled so far to be here. I can't leave you at the airport like that.

Ext. In a senior home in California. Pia, Richard uncle's Sol, and his wife are sitting around a swimming pool.

Pia

This is a nice place.

Uncle Sol

Yes, it is very good for senior people like us. There are apartments around the swimming pool. People can socialize when they step out of their homes. Our apartments have own kitchen to cook whatever we like. And we can eat food made by the center kitchen, as well. We have both social live, privacy and freedom.

Pia

I appreciate that you allowed us to visit you. You don't know me, and you are just Richard's great-uncle. You hardly know Richard but you are concerned for him. He desperately needs his father's attentions, or he will have a psychiatric problem.

Uncle Sol

I am just a few years older than his father. We grew up together just like brothers. I know everything about his marriages. I am sorry for things ending up like this. Richard suffered a lot, living between his parents. His mother was saying bad things against his father. You are a nice girl. I hope you can help him overcome this situation.

Ext. In front of a restaurant. Sydney, at seventy, shaking Pia's hand. Next to them is Richard. Ext. Inside the restaurant, Sydney has a smile on his face.

Sydney

It is whose idea to put your marriage statement in the NY Times ad?

Pia

It was Richard's idea. I thought no one would read those small ads. It was there for just three days, and we waste three hundred dollars for that.

Sydney

It is not a waste. One of my clients caught that and congratulated me. I was happy then. Hope our relationship will improve from now on. It once was so bad. Richard broke the window glass of my car, wrote letters to threaten my clients, and use phone calls to disturb people who have a relationship with me. If Uncle Sol didn't insist to see you guys and convince me, we might not have had the chance to see each other.

Richard

Dad, I was wrong to act like that. All I hope is to see you again. You know I love you very much. I do whatever to catch your attention.

Pia

Thank you for forgiving us. He acts like a child, rolling on the floor, asking for candy. He doesn't know the others' feelings and doesn't know how to work things out. You know, he was exploding and even hit me for no reason every time when he thought of you. I didn't stop him to do those things because I thought that might help him to release his anger. We have no money to see the psychologist.

Sydney

Why did you think of visiting Uncle Sol? Are you on the way to Mexico, check my divorce record with your mother?

Richard

No, just by phone, I found out that your divorce record had already been filed in Mexico's court. I am a genius on this kind of investigation. I even made the man send me the record. That divorce was considered legal in New York in those days. My mother has no grounds to sue you and spend money like that. I am the one who suggested to see Uncle Sol. She took me to take the airplane, the first time I fly.

Sydney

You know your mother does not believe that divorce is legal. All these years, she double-endorsed all the checks I paid for child-support and gave that to the lawyers. That is why I stop pay her sometimes. She took me to court, make things happen ugly and painful. She doesn't know to handle money. That is why I kept her salary when we were married and make investments. You don't know that I work so hard is all for our family, and you don't appreciate it.

Richard

Dad, I'll tell you good news. Pia got pregnant.

Sydney

Really, I will be a grand pap again? Pia, it is a serious decision to choose to be a mother. You not only need to carry him, give birth to him, and financially support him. You have to make him happy and healthy. There will be problems if you can't meet the requirements.

Pia

Okay. I know what you mean. Don't worry, I will reconsider it carefully.

Ext. At Pia and Richard's apartment. Richard points at Pia's stomach

Richard

When will you get rid of that thing? It seems my father doesn't care about him.

Ext. After a few months, Pia, Richard, and Sydney are at a restaurant.

Sydney

How are your guys?

Richard

We are fine, as well as our baby. He is a male.

Sydney has a big smile on his face and turns to Pia.

Sydney

You still kept the baby? You said you will reconsider what I said. I thought you also believe it's not easy to raise a baby and choose to get rid of him. You look so skinny I cannot tell you are still carrying him.

Pia

This is my child. I will keep him no matter what.

Sydney hides his happiness.

Thank you for keeping my grandson. I care about him but hope you to consider the whole situation seriously.

Ext. Pia is at the hospital alone. Her baby is born. Sydney shows up. He runs to the window glass where can see the new born infants from the other room. He looks so eagerly, can't wait to see his grandson. Richard walks in with dirt on his face.

Sydney

Where were you? You were not around when your wife was giving birth to your baby?

Richard

I just went to the library. I found the number of the ship that took Grandpa to the United States. It is amazing that there is a paper list of all the passengers' names on the ship. See, this is the record with Grandpa and grandma's record, you not curious?

Richard raises a sheet of paper and has a big smile on his face where has obvious dirty. He looks like a child discovering something valuable.

Pia

You have not asked a word about your son yet.

Richard

How is he? I will be not your baby from now on, right?

Sydney

Richard, you are someone's father now. You are not a baby. Pia and Sydney look at each other. They both feel confuse and sorry for Richard's respond.

Ext. At Pia and Richard's apartment. A photographer takes pictures of the baby, Lewis who looks maturely at his seven weeks old. Pia suggests taking one picture for the whole family. Those pictures are so nice that Pia decides to keep them for $300, which is half of her monthly salary. In front of the photographer. Richard hits Pia and kicks her even though she fell on the floor,

Richard

How can you keep those pictures for three hundred dollars? They are so expensive, equal to your half month's rent.

The Photographer was shot by what happened. He holds Richard and Richard run out of the apartment.

Pia

Don't worry, I need those pictures. He will say sorry when he come back and beg for my pardons.

Ext. In a quiet corner of a hospital. Sydney, Pia, and Richard are sitting in the waiting area. Richard is filling out a form. He uses a pen to scratch the form angrily all of a sudden. Later, Sydney and Richard are called into a room. Pia is holding Lewis, waiting outside. Later, a person who looks like a doctor talk to Pia.

Doctor

According to our diagnosis, your husband has a serious mental problem. He is very angry. We would like to keep him as an in- patient in the hospital but must get your permission first.

Pia

Is that so serious? I don't think his is schizophrenia. It looks like he is a child who never grew up and his life environment made him angry. If we have more patience and be warm to him, he could be turn peaceful. I prefer to take him home and help him to live in a normal world.

Ext. At a restaurant, four of them, Richard, Pia, Lewis and Sydney, sit at a table for afternoon tea.

Sydney

Richard, you must treat your wife nicely. The rest of your life will be controlled by her.

Richard

I know what you mean. She can send me to a mental hospital just like you did to your first wife. I am not so stupid to let you handle my life.

Pia looks frustrated.

Pia

I don't know what to do now. I always believe any problem has its solution. I never expected the situation can be so difficult. I can't even protect myself. How can I protect my son?

Lewis's hand moves and is burned by the hot bottle. He is crying. Sydney asks to hold him. He holds him tight, kisses him again and again. Sydney was very upset.

Sydney

Richard, don't ever think of walking away from your family. You have your child and wife now. It's your responsibility to stay with them.

Voice in the Movies

This is the last time they gather together.

Ext. Richard talks on the phone; on the other side is his father.

Richard

I have to stay away from you because you plan to send me to a mental hospital. My mother said you were supposed to send me to a law school, and you send me to a mental hospital.

Sydney

Don't go, please. I will see Lewis and you every week from now on. Must be three of you together. I work so hard to bring up our family to the middle class. You will destroy all my effort if you walk away like that.

Richard murmurs, grabs some of his stuff, and bangs the door behind him.

Voice

Richard ran away before his son's first birthday. Sydney did not visit his grandson but sent him a one-hundred-dollar check with a signature sign seriously. Pia made a copy of that check before cashing it and dropped the copy into a drawer. She didn't notice that that check was there for twenty-five years, and even though the drawer was moved here and there. It is that signature that made her start the case because it is obviously different from the signature on the will.

Three years later.

Ext. In a garden, Sydney; his third wife, Teresa; and Kenny's children are sitting around. Next to them are food and vegetables. Sydney is reading a book to the children. He is very patient, and his eyes show a lot of love.

Sydney

This is how Israel set up their country. Two thousand years ago, our great-great-great . . . parents traveled for a long, long way and escaped from the enemies who tortured us. Jews lost our homeland and lived in all over the world. My family were in Russia, but we still remember we are Jews. We care about our family first, as well as care about our country.

Kenny shows up in the scene.

Kenny

Daddy, I received a very horrible letter from Richard. This is the third time I received this kind of letter.

Sydney

What is that about?

Kenny

In one of those letters, he said, "My friend asked for a payment to pick up your children from their school at the end of the day." Last letter, he said " I had a dream: students in Professor.

Fishman's classroom are screaming. They see Professor Fishman is lying on the floor, with blood spilling out". He obviously is threatening my family and wants to destroy my life. My friend, a professional analyzes Richard's letters and said he has serious schizophrenia. I have to stay away from him. I hope you take the same position. If you don't end contact with him, we will end contact with you.

Sydney

Ending contact with him still cannot stop him from bothering you. He is autistic not schizophrenia. Autistic people do not know how to deal with people. He can't project himself to the others and understand the others' feelings. He's just liked a child saying that for fun. He does not mean to do that.

Kenny

He is crazy. End contact with him. You still can see me and my children. Otherwise, you will lose all of us. I am serious. I can't put my family under tight monitors of a crazy guy.

Sydney

Please don't force me to make such a decision. I have kept my promise to you and end the marriage with his mother. That hurt him a lot. He has autism. If he has parents around him, he can have a decent life in a certain field. He was a chess champion in the New York junior high school. I always feel guilty that I couldn't give him a healthy growing environment.

Kenny

You didn't give me a decent growing environment neither. You put my mother into a mental hospital. I have no home. I grew up in different relatives' homes. Start from twelve years old, I lived in school's boardinghouse.

Ext. Go back to Kenny's 14 years old. Kenny sitting on a swing, watching students picked up by their parents for summer vacation. They are cheerful and run to their father. Kenny has tears in his eyes.

Ext. Students are back, happy to mention their experience at home in the summer vacation Kenny sits next and had nothing to say.

Kenny

When other children couldn't wait to go home before summer vacation, I have nowhere to go. When they talked about their family after coming back to the school, I had nothing to say. I don't have a home, I don't have a mother, and I don't have a father. It is not easy to set up my family. I finally get one and I can't watch it be destroyed. We must stay away from Richard and you.

Sydney

I financially supported you all these years. I feel proud of you. You finished college at seventeen years old and finished a PhD degree at a top college. Can you give me one more chance? We can call the policeman and arrest Richard. We can stop him with a court order.

Kenny

I don't care. All I care is protect my children from being threaten by your lovely son, Richard. If you not end the relationship with him, I will end the relationship with you.

Ext. Outside the court: Sydney and Kenny

Kenny

I am sorry. You see now, the case you filed for grandpa's right for visiting my children is denied by the judge already. They don't think you have a right to visit us when you keep contact with Richard, a crazing guy. Your better leave us alone, you can consider you have only one son, Richard.

Sydney

I have something left for your children that I prepared for many years.

Kenny

We don't need anything. You know, after I pay off the 7 percent interest- rate mortgage that you offer me, I don't think maintaining the relationship with you is important anymore. You take care. Bye-bye, Dad.

Sydney

You can't get mad for the 7 percent you paid me because the interest rates the bank charge then is 15%. I will file a case in court, to stop Richard. Don't go, please. Richard is autistic and his life is sad enough. Abandoning him will make him more craze.

Kenny

That is your problem. Too bad, you have a crazy son. Kenny looks at Sydney straightly to his eyes, pats his shoulder, turns around, and walks away.

Ext. In front of Pia's apartment Richard rings Pia's doorbell and asks for help.

Richard

Can you go to the court with me? My father and Kenny are taking me to court

Pia

What did you do again? Kenny didn't contact you all these years. You must have done something to offend him.

Richard

I don't know. You go or not go. If you go, you just need to sit there and say nothing.

Ext. In a courtroom. Pia is sitting aside and watching Richard stand in front of the judge. Sydney and Kenny do not show up. There are two lawyers. One represents Richard. After a while, Richard comes back.

Richard

It is okay now. We can go home now. I am fine. I don't expect that my father hired a lawyer to defend me as well. He didn't mean to send me to jail. He just wanted to give me a lesson. The lawyer said I lost my mind when I did things. The judge let me go. I will not bother Kenny any more.

Pia

What did you do? I want to know.

Richard

I wrote some letter. Just put things in words without signature. They still caught me. I will not do that again. I will not bother you again. Bye-bye!

The screen shows: three years later.

Ext. Richard ring bell again in front of Pia's apartment. He looks tire weak and has strong smell.

Richard

Could you help me, please? My mother was sent to a nursing home in upstate New York. She can't pay rent for me anymore and we lost our apartment.

Pia

How come things happen like that? (Pia searches Richard's bag.) Look at that dirty and old bread. Is that your food? You smell so bad. Is that shit on your pants? Did you just step out from your apartment or you lost it for days?

Richard

I have been hanging out in the street for a few days. Richard described what happened in the last few days

Ext. Richard holding a bag, during day he bought an order and sitting at a McDonald' all day. At night, he is sitting in an emergency room of a hospital. He opens a bag and takes out a piece of old bread. He eats part of it and throws the rest back to his bag where he has different kinds of garbage. He is dirty, smelly, and tired.

Ext. In the corner of a street, Richard is stopped by a Black guy, a robber.

The robber

Don't move! Give me what you have to me.

The robber grasp Richard's bag and takes Richard's wallet, in which has all Richard's IDs. He then throws the bag back to Richard. Richard is scare, angry and doesn't know what to say.

Pia listens what Richard and not believe.

Are you serious? You hang out in the street all these days? How can you survive? You always tell lie.

Richard looks scare and change his mind.

I am sorry, I come here from my ardent. I can't stay there anymore because we couldn't pay rent. She was in a mental hospital and from there she was transfer to a senior home in upstate. They took all her money.

Ext. In the serious storm, Pia and Richard walk in a street. When they reach Richard's apartment, they see the door was sealed by two long sheets of paper that have the court's stamp date at one week ago. Pia holds Richard and cry.

Pia

How can they throw you to the street in the storm like that? When you handle your life, your IQ is just like a child. How come they threw a child to the street?

Richard

They put my mother in a nursing room in upstate. It takes two hours on bus to get there. When I visit her, I can take a shower but was not allowed to stay there for overnight. Every time my mother watches me leave; she knows that means I will sleep in the street. She cries a lot. She said it is Sydney put her there and she dares not ask to leave.

Pia

Let me take care of this thing!

Ext. In the bus, Pia spits out a lot. She is carsick. After a heavy snow the streets are blocked, and it takes four hours to get the senior home where Glady locates. In the front desk, Pia argues with a man who looks like the manager of there.

Pia

I am from New York City. It took four hours to travel here today. Why do you keep this lady far away from his son? Are you sure that is her choice?

Manager

She was transferred here from a hospital, and she never asks to leave. you have no right to take her out. I have to call a policeman for your disturbance.

Ext. A few policemen walk in. They review Pia's passport and say nothing.

Pia

My last name is same as this lady, and I am her daughter-in-law. I know this woman very much. In her mind, her son is more important than her own life. She won't leave her son alone and watch him live in the street like that. She would rather die to protect her son.

When Pia says that Gladys cries loudly.

Gladys

My son must travel a few hours to visit me here. Every time I watch him step out of my room and become a homeless my heart is broken. I have enough money to pay rent. You force me to stay here and make me use all my $2500 pension to pay you. You throw my son to the street and cut my heart piece by piece. I dare not say no because it is my husband arrange all these things. He is a powerful man that is why I dare not say no to you.

Glady cries loudly again.

Pia

It has nothing to do with Sydney, if you don't want to stay here, you can go back to New York with me.

Pia looks a policeman. The Policemen look at each other

Policemen talk to the manager

By law you have to let her go. Glady, Richard and Pia landing into a taxi.

Ext. In a small motel room in New York City: Richard, Pia, and Gladys, who has some stuff with her.

Pia

You can live here tonight. This is a family motel. They charge $40 a night for a room with a private bathroom. You can simply cook outside at the kitchen; The rent is $1,200 a month and your pension can cover it. I have paid the deposit and two days rent already plus the taxi fee from upstate to here.

Ext. Next day at the motel.

Gladys

Thank you very much. I dare not say no to those people who kept me there. I thought they are sent by Sydney. Sydney is powerful. When the bank opens on Monday, I will pay you back all the money you spent for us.

Pia

I have a friend selling her studio for $35,000. The size is same as my apartment and is in the same building. I know you can offer to buy it, and I can take care of your guys easily there. The maintenance is just $245, better than you paying $1,200 a month to rent a room here.

Gladys

This is the money I owe you. Pick that up, and get out of my face. I don't need your advice. We are fine now. Don't ever think about my money.

Gladys starts cursing, looks angry. She pushes Pia out of the room and bangs the door. Richard says nothing.

Screen shows two years later

Ext. At the same family-style motel.

Motel Owner

You are the one who put them here. The lady has disappeared for a week. No one pays the rent. This man can't take care of himself at all. You must take him away from here.

Richard

My mother is in a nursing home again. This time she is in New York City, Rego Park. They don't allow me to visit her. They said I am taking an old lady's money and said I am crazy.

Ext. At a lobby of a nursing home. Gladys is sitting with Richard, Pia, and a few social workers.

Social Worker

Gladys, we will not let your son visit you so often. Every time he comes, he asks for money and abuses you. You are a senior person, we have right to protect you.

Gladys

Oh, poor Richard, he is just like a little boy. He cannot take care of himself. He never works in his life and he doesn't know how to cook. He needs money and he needs my help, but I am old. I can't carry him anymore.

Gladys talks and then screams louder and louder. She stands in front of Richard, keeps touching his face, and cries.

Gladys

They will not let you visit me. I can't see you anymore.

Richard showing no responds, has the expression that an autistic person usually has.

The social worker drags Gladys away from Richard. Gladys keeps screaming.

Pia

Don't worry! I know your situation. I will take care of him. Even though he has withdrawn his share, the ten thousand dollars, from my apartment. He ran away from us and never pay child support; however, I will take him home.

Ext. In Pia' neighborhood, Richard hangs out in the street with long hair, looks like he lost his mind. A few children laugh at his face and then run after Lewis, Pia's seventeen-year-old son.

Child

Lewis! This is your dad. You know, yesterday he gave us a one- dollar bill. He once gave twenty dollars to people who he didn't know. You have a rich and nice father. Hahaha!

Ext. At Pia's home. Lewis is searching the refrigerator. He then run to Richard

Lewis

I lost the yoga I had from my job. Must be you take it. You never paid child support and now lives in my home and make me being humiliated. You hit my mother when I was small. I am growing up now, I must get you today.

Lewis runs to Richard before Pia realizes what happen. He is on top of Richard and keeps punching him seriously.

Ext. In the street, Richard meets Lewis. He jumps over a car and runs away desperately.

Ext. In Pia's apartment. Richard holds a sharp knife, murmuring as he walks into the room. Pia is leaning on the window and has no way to go backward.

Richard

I am not afraid of Lewis… I am not afraid of Lewis. Richard is walking to Pia and points a knife to her.

Richard

Do you see these blue and black marks? It is your son who made it. I will get you today as return.

Richard waves the knife. Pia uses her hands to stop him and bleeds. Richard is shot, and Pia runs away at that moment. She runs down to the entrance of the building and sits down on the stairs and cries. Policemen come, and the ambulance comes soon, as well.

Ext. In the emergency room. Pia covers her palm and cry loudly. She watches the bleed come down a lot a lot and nobody come up to help her till the blood stop. Finally, a doctor shown up.

Doctor

I can only saw it quickly. You need to come back. You get hurt seriously. You have to stay here overnight. Nobody tells me to come.

Ext. In the courtroom. Two prosecutors sit with Pia.

Prosecutor

Look at your thumb. In that small area, it received twelve stiches. It is almost cut off by Richard. If you don't get it sutured immediately, you will be disabled all your life. This is enough to prosecute him for the injury.

Pia

He lost his mind, and his IQ is just like a child in some way. He doesn't know how to deal with people, and he doesn't know to consider the others' feelings. I will not prosecute him but will divorce him. I can't carry him anymore. Please take care of him for me.

Ext. In a hospital room Pia and Richard sitting there with a few social workers.

Pia

I am sorry I have to divorce with Richard. He is dangers. I dare not stay in a same household with him anymore. Since he can't go out of the hospital at this moment, we need you as a witness and give me a public notary for the divorce paper.

Staff

Richard, you don't against her decision, do you?

Richard

I am sorry Pia. I know I have no choice I listen to you

Pia and Richard both cry.

Pia

I will keep touch with you, will visit you once a while.

Voice

Pia divorced with Richard. The court did not prosecute him but order him to receive psychiatric treatment. He must stay in the hospital for six months. During that time, his mother got sick.

Ext. Gladys is in bed and crying weakly.

Gladys

I want to see my son. I want to be sure everything is good for him.

Gladys misses Richard a lot. She keeps calling his name but has no way to contact him. She was unable to see Richard till she died. For that reason, she keeps her eyes open.

Ext. Inside a Chinese fast-food restaurant, Pia meets Richard.

Richard

It is luck that they didn't keep me in that hospital for ever. I am not crazy. I just have bad temper when I don't know how to deal with people and don't know how to express myself. I remember you once complain that every time we see each other you are the one who pay for the expenses. You hope I can pay once a while. I don't mind to end contact since I have no money pay for you.

Pia

I just hope to see your appreciation. Let us keep touch for you don't have any family members or friends in this world. Remember you still have me. For the sake of your poor crazy mother, I will keep an eye on you. Let me know if you need something. Please keep in touch.

Chapter 6

SYDNEY'S TESTAMENT AND A "PROBATE WILL"

Ext. Sydney, Diana, and Ana are walking into an apartment of New York, Manhattan, Lawyer Curtain's office and home. They shake each other.

Curtain

Welcome, Mr. Fishman. This is . . . (Curtain turns to Diana.)

Diana

I am the niece of Teresa. My uncle is ninety-six years old and could not see. He needs some help. That is why we are here. This is the first time I meet you, but I did hear about you when the first two wills were made.

Curtain

I am sorry. This office is small and set up at because I have already retired. The living room is the waiting area, and Sydney wants you to stay here.

Ext. Sydney and Curtain sitting in the office.

Sydney

I come to alter my will because my wife has passed away. I don't need to give her 50 percent of my assets anymore. I am going to give most of my money to my grandchildren and to donate 40 percent to city colleges, just as my first will indicated.

Curtain

I know that. Your second will gave 50 percent to Teresa and after Teresa die her inheritance from you will only go to Victor, her nephew. Why would you make that changed?

Sydney

Actually, I altered my first will because I was under dressed. I was blind and many times I need to rely on Terisa. For that reason, her niece unduly influences her and force me to give 50 percent of my assets to her. Now she died, and I have the right to take everything back. I know Palmer will be very upset about that. That is why I keep them outside. I am sorry. They have no blood relationship with me, and I hardly meet them all these years. The most important reason is that I still very much love my family. My father died before I was born and I know how sad it is without a father. I worked so hard all my life actually is for my children and grandchildren.

Curtain

I understand your position. I have to get the documents ready. Those are your money. You have the right to give it to anybody. Today if a wife needs to share 50% of her husband's asset, she has to file a court case first. How much a wife can get determines by her functions in the family, if she has children, if she helps accumulate the family asset. You and Teresa had no children and all the money are made by you. You absolute has right to arrange your money. All you need is to sign your will in front of two witnesses. My wife and my neighbor Susan can help us to process it.

Sydney

Thank you I am glad that beside the donation all my money will go to my children and grandchildren. I finally let them know that how hard I work for them and how much I love them! You know it is not easy to stay alive for a blind man. Don't let anybody see this will. Only you and me keep a copy

Curtain

How much money do you leave to them? In your previous wills, you used percent, and the total amount you mentioned was less than one hundred thousand dollars.

Sydney

I prefer to keep it as a secret. You will know it when the day comes. Please just base on the percent, as my first will said.

Six months before Sydney pass away.

Ext. Sydney is talking on telephone with broker Jeffry from Vanguard.

Jeffry

Good morning. Mr. Fishman. The document for your power of attorney is ready. Diana Palmer will be in charge all of your four accounts, which involve seven million dollars.

Sydney

No! No! That is not what I want. She can sign checks for only one account. I let her involve because I can't see.

Jeffry

Mr. Fishman, according to the rule in Vanguard, when we add an agent, it's done at the account level, not at the fund level. That means if you name Diana as your agent, she will be able to touch all the funds under your accounts.

Sydney

Well, well, I mean, that puts me at a disadvantage, I mean, she had— she has access to all of my accounts, and I could be dispossessed if I have an argument with her or anything. I want to limit her to one account. Is there any way that can be done? I mean, can I shift that account to another title?

Jeffry

Let me find a way to solve the problem. Okay, my supervisor said we'll limit her power to only one account. You don't have to worry now.

Voice from the Movie

This conversation occurred after Sydney alters his will and a half year before he died. It is obvious that he was not intended to give all his money to Palmer family at all. He didn't consider they are his family member and he tried to control his money back desperately.

Six months later, right after Sydney is dead.

Ext. In Curtain's office. Teresa's sister Olga and her child, Diana, are shaking hands with Curtain.

Diana

We know each other when I sent Sydney to alter his will one year ago. My uncle Sydney just passed away. We hope to know if he left anything to us.

Curtain

I am sorry. He eliminated all you and your children's names in his last will. By law he has the right to do it. He said your aunt passed away and had no right to share his assets anymore. All his money will go back to the Fishman family and the charity.

Your aunt did leave all her asset to you and choose Sydney as the executor of her will. I wonder why one year after her died he still not release her money to you. Do you get along well? Now I can let you have your aunt's assets, not Sydney's.

Diana

I know we will have my aunt's money. How about Sydney's money. Do you mean my aunt married him for forty years and got nothing from her marriage?

Curtain

He mentioned that all his monies were made by himself, most of them were accumulate before he married your aunt. He allowed your aunt kept all her income, annually thirty thousand dollars as the book keeper from a church. When he allowed your aunt keep 50% of his asset, he didn't ask you aunt give him the same deal. He let all your aunt's money go straight to you. By law he has the right to handle his assets particularly when your aunt died before him and they don't have children.

Diana

My aunt considered we are her children.

Curtain

That is a different story. If he loved her and respected her wishes, he should have left something to your guys. It does surprise me that his assets are worth ten million dollars and he left nothing to your guys.

Diana

I don't care. My aunt said all the money she had from him will belong to her nieces and nephew. She is twelve years younger than him. All of a sudden, she got cancer. Even then, she should have been able to live longer than him, but a doctor's treatments made her die in three months.

Ext. Sydney's spirit and an angel watch what they are talking.

Sydney's Spirit

I also wonder, how come I live longer than her? I have already given up when I made the second will. I don't like Diana who wanted my money so desperately. She undue influenced Teresa to challenge my first will and forced me to pay her 50% of my money. For punishing Diana, I order the money Treasa took from me must go to Victor only. Nobody can probate my will except Teresa.

Ext. Back to Curtain's office

The Angel

It is your second wife, Gladys, who made Teresa get cancer and die before you. In the second will, you meant to spread your ashes wherever. Do you know why you changed your mind in the last will and wished to be buried at "Beth David Cemetery"? That was also Gladys's interfering because she was buried there already. This is not a coincidence. Life is destined. You hated each other and lost contact for many years, but you are buried together in the same cemetery.

Diana

We need all Sydney's ten million dollars assets! If you help us get that, we will give you two million dollars. You know Sydney did contact Fishman family members for more than twenty years. His older son doesn't care about his money, and the younger son is crazy. They know nothing about how he thinks and they have no witnesses to challenge us. They have no choice but accept our arrangement. They might even get no chance to object to the will we probated. Two million dollars is much more than what you saved in your whole life. You have retired now and you don't have to worry that your behavior might destroy your care. Two million dollar can help you buy a property for your family, not live in a rental apartment like this.

Curtain

What do you want me to do?

Diana

Take a look at this instrument. This is Sydney told you how to distribute his asset.

Diana displays a note composed by big words, a few names and each of them were attach with number.

Curtain

Where did you get it? its stroke is strong, tidy and identical.

Diana

These names are picked up from Sydney's letter. I used the copy and paste key in the computer to make this note. The number are the provisions in the new will.

Curtain

The letters are too big and it doesn't look like written by a ninety-six years old blind man.

Diana continued

I must put the words in this size because he can't read and write words in typing. Don't worry they are 100% of Sydney's handwriting, No one can challenge it, not even a handwriting expert. This will be the only document back up the provisions in the will:

Olga Palme	20
Diana Palmer	40
Anata M. Garzon	10
Víctor Palmer	20
Cynthia Palmer	10

Curtain

This instrument did not mention anything about Will and had no dollar sign. Those number can mean apple, orange but not %.

Diana

I know what you mean. It was not easy to pick up and copy word by word from his hand writing paper to make up this piece of note. We don't have time to make it perfect. You are the only will draft deal with him. As long as you say Sydney handed this instrument to you orally and tell you base on this to alter his will nobody can challenge it.

We then make up a page only list the will provisions. I will make an initial on it to substitute the page that with his wished provisions. In this way we can still keep his signature in the last page of the will but get everything we want.

Ext. Curtain pulls out the will page on his computer. He adjusts some words in the second page and makes the first page listing only the provisions provided by Diana. For convenience he didn't eliminate the lines related to donations.

Curtain

I kept the donation content because it saves a lot of changes. However, I put $500 each for three of his donations and deleted the 10 percent to 15 percent that he wished. Those fingers are big if basing on his ten million dollars asset.

Diana

For your convenience it is OK to keep that. However, all of us hope to add something on his will. My aunt died before him and put us into such a bad situation. We take that as a lesson and want to mention how our inherit ant go in case, we predecease him.

Curtain

He was ninety-six years old, and your guys are in your fifties. It sounds weird that he even worries about how his money goes if your guys die before him.

Diana

Anything could happen. Just consider we are your clients, and do what we want you to do.

The Voice in the Movies
(voice is raised)

If Olga Palmer predeceases me, her 20 percent in my residuary estate will go to Victor Palmer Sr.If Diana Palmer predeceases me, her 35 percent in my residuary estate will be shared in equal percentages to her husband, David, and each of their three children, with David acting as trustee of the shares left to their children until they reach majority.

If Victor Palmer Jr. predeceases me, his 20 percent in my residuary estate will go to Olga Palmer.

If Cynthia Palmer predeceases me, her 15 percent will be shared in equal shares to each of her children, per stripes.

If Ana Maria Garzon Yepez predeceases me, her 10 percent will go to her heirs….

Ext. In Curtain's office, Curtain and Diana are there. Curtain is handing a paper to Diana.

A Ten Million $ Testament

Curtain

As what you requested, all your provisions are in a single paper now. Diana receives the update page, holds her breath, and make an initial S carefully on the corner of it. The screen enlarges the S she made.

Diana

S for Sydney. Ha, ha, ha, ha.

Curtain

Should I say you gave me this instrument?

Diana

Of course not. You must say Sydney is the only one who handed this instrument to you and handed it in oral. For avoiding more questions, you will say no witnesses was present at the moment. By the way, none Palmer know Sydney gave them such inheriting. We didn't involve the will sign at all.

Curtain

We don't have witnesses, video tape, or audio tape to record the process. Do you think the instrument you made up and my affidavit is enough to support the ten million dollars testament?

Diana

As a will drafter, if you swore and insist something nobody can challenge it. The law requests people who reject the will submit proofs not the beneficiaries. We are always being well protected because American laws tend to support the will because that means respecting the deceased's wishes. That is why people who challenge wills can hardly win. Fishman's family didn't contact each other for over twenty years, they can never prove that the provisions in the will are not Sydney's intention.

Besides that, they only have one month to challenge us. Before they respond it, the time is expired..

Curtain

Looks like you all rely on what I say.

Diana

Just say a few words you can make two million dollars. Isn't that worth it?

Ext. Sydney's spirit and the angel watch all they did. Sydney is very angry and worried.

Sydney's Spirit

They really take action now. I didn't trust Diana all these years and kept her away from my businesses. I didn't trust Curtain, as well, and that is why I did not even tell him how much assets I have. I thought as a lawyer he dares not to change my will because that against law. I can't imagine that they commit crimes so easily

Angel

Now we have to get help from your ex-daughter-in-law. She is the only one who can give you a hand. Everything is predestined including her marriage. She is pretty and smart, but I made her marry your autistic son within eight days. That made her suffering a lot. She divorces with your son and register in a dating internet. I will block her see if she contacts your son again.

Chapter 7
CHALLENGE THE PROBATE WILL

Ext. Pia is waiting on the street. A car stops in front of her. A guy, Kan, comes out from the driver seat and open the car door for her. He is gentleman.

Kan

Wow. It is so traffic. I never experienced such a traffic in my life. I almost want to return home. From my home to here, it usually takes forty-five minutes of driving; today I spent more than three hours on the road.

Pia

I prefer you couldn't come. I am very very sick now. It is weird that I am very dizzy all of a sudden. I never had that kind of feeling in my life.

Kan

Since I've already here let us go eat something. Do you know any good restaurant for a vegetarian?

Pia

There is one seems good. I didn't go there for a while. Hope it is still as good as before.

Ext. After sitting down in the restaurant, Pia and Kan notice that there are no other customers except them. The restaurant even doesn't turn all the lights on, and most of the place is dark. Kan says nothing during the dinner.

Pia

I am sorry, I haven't come to this restaurant for a while. Before, it is very busy. I don't know why they are so slow now.

Two months later.

Ext. In Kan's apartment. Kan is very happy and is making tomato soup.

Pia

This is the food I like. The restaurant near my office makes this beef with broccoli very well. I hope can share that with you.

Kan

I am sorry I don't eat meat. The food you bought; I can't take it.

Pia eats her own food in silence and she so hope Kan can taste the beef she likes. As Kan requested, Pia took many nice clothes with her and wears them one by one, like a fashion model. Kan is very impressed and excited about how she looks on those clothes. He takes picture from different angle, takes pictures for Pia one by one.

Kan

What, it is so wire! All the pictures I took disappeared from my iPhone. It never happened like that. Also, I have a bad headache.

For the rest of night, Kan is very down. Pia wants to go home by bus on the same night. Kan insists on sending her to the bus terminal, but he is not familiar with the road. His car turns from left and right and makes Pia have very bad carsickness. For the headache he has Kan feels he is in hell, as well.

Ext. Pia is talking to her business partner, Sherly, on the phone.

Pia

It's strange that people I like on the dating website were live or move to the other states all of a sudden. The nearest one is in NJ, and every time we dated, either him or me was physically sick. It looks like something is blocking me. Maybe I should get off the website. Maybe Richard still needs me.

Sherly

Good! Stop making those silly dating. Let us go to a concert. A symphony orchestra from China will have a show in Kennedy Hall this week. We can go to enjoy it. It just like we save a trip to China.

Pia

Fine. I can go straight there from my office at Thursday night and save a trip from Queen in the weekend. I am lazy; for 35 years in New York City, I never go to concerts of Broadway shows.

Sherly

Come on! Let us have a dinner in Chinatown on Saturday and then go to the concert. We can consider that as a shareholders' meeting. We never have one since we purchased that building. Our investment is successful and we need a celebration.

Ext. Sydney and Angle were around

Angle

That is the only concert Pia has in Kennedy Hall and that is the only dinner the shareholders had. I am the one who arranged that.

Sydney's spirit

Does it have something to do with the court case? How can the meeting help us?

Angle

You will see. One of the shareholders is Pia's brother-in-law, who is also a lawyer. He will make one important document for us. Without that, Pia wouldn't start the court case when Richard collapsed and refused to cooperate.

Ext. Outside of a library, Pia is waiting for Richard and watching him run out from the library with a big smile.

Richard

Tell you an important news. My father has already passed away. I called the Social Security department and found that out. I have also checked; he left no will. That means as his son, I can get 30 percent of his assets automatically. I will give you and Lewis's 50 percent if you help me get that.

Pia

His wife will automatically get his asset. We have no chance to step in.

Richard

I just know that his wife died one year ago. So, it is easy for us to claim his money.

Pia

This can be a big project. How about if there is a will and someone else also claims his money? If I have to spend legal fees to fight for that, I must make sure to have my investment back? How can I trust you if you walk away with the money?

Richard

I will write you a paper tied up by legal power.

Ext. In a restaurant at Chinatown: Pia; Richard; Pia's sister Yin and her husband, Bob; Pia's nephew Seamon; and Sherly.

Yin

This is the legal paper Bob prepared for you. You are lucky to have that right away because of this dinner. We have not seen each other for almost a year, have we?

Pia

It is interesting. I meant to go to the concert on Thursday. Sherly insisted go on Saturday and by happen, I know I need this document yesterday, Friday.

Richard

I will have it notarized tomorrow. I have the IDs that the public notary needs. They are student ID and food-stamp ID.

Pia

What? You were in Hunter College thirty years ago. How can they accept that kind of ID? You will apply for a passport anyway. Let us wait for the passport to come.

Richard

No! No! Don't wait. They just need IDs with picture. Tomorrow you take a day off, and I promise give you a legal paper back up what I said.

(Richard always listens to Pia, but he insisted his opinion and they both don't know that is the only chance Pia got Richard's notify promise.)

Ext. Sydney and Angel are around

Angel

Look! The shareholders' meeting gives them a chance to set up an agreement and without that Pia doesn't challenge the will. Altogether they take three days to get things ready and that is the only three days they have.

There was an interesting coincident at the night after shareholders' dinner.

Ext. Camara shows the shareholders are on a subway platform after dinner.

Share holder Seamon (Pia's nephew)

We still have time. Let us see Richard get into his subway cart first, then we go to the concern.

That is Pia never do because she knows Richard is familiar to NY subway. Since the shareholders willing to do it, Pia follows with them.

Angel talk to Sydney's spirit

Every little thing is arranged by me. If they did send Richard to the platform that night Pia will never get a chance to ask if Lewis' name was also mentioned in Sydney's will and without that information, she will not start the case when Richard is absent. Richard is collapse before the dead line. You will see how difficult they file the rejection in the court.

Time: one day after.

Ext. Pia and Richard meet in a park of Chinatown again. Richard looks horrible. Her beard is long, and his eyes are hollow. He looks so weak and can collapse anytime. They sit down at the park, eating two takeout orders that Pia bought.

Richard

There is a will! The will drafter came to my adult home yesterday. He showed me a will with my father's signature. He said my father left nothing to me because of those pictures that I holding guns. I am done. He said I was arrested then because of that. My father never forgives me and leaves me nothing. I am done.

Pia

Does that signature look like your father's signature?

Richard

Yes, it is! I am familiar with that. I also go to the court. this morning. It did have my father's will probated there. We have only one month for appeal. If we don't file objection in time, the money will automatically belong to them. Those are nieces and nephew of his third wife.

Pia

Can you object the will as his son?

Richard

Yes. But the chance I win is low. He can give his money to anybody, even to a dog. I did not contact my father for twenty after I sending those pictures. You know I did that because nobody helps me to find a job. I have no income. I thought he will give me some money when he sees I have gun. I am stupid. The estate he had is ten million dollars. I should have kept a nice relationship with him. He always told me he works hard for me. My mother did not allow me to keep touch with him. She hated him.

Pia

You never growth up. You don't know how to communicate with people because you don't know the others feel. You like a child, for having candy, roll on the floor. You are accepting mental treatment under court order. Maybe we can use that as a reason to cancel the pictures and object that will. Law never holds responsibility to people who are mentally ill.

Richard looks very angry all of a sudden.

Richard

I have to go. I am done. I don't want to claim money as a mental patient. You will send me to mental hospital and I will never have chance to spend those money.

Richard was angry and Pia runs after him to the subway platform where they were in the previous night. Before Richard walks into the train, Pia asks a question.

Pia

Did your father mention Lewis?

Richard

Yes.

Ext. In Pia's apartment. Pia and her son, Lewis.

Pia

Your father doesn't answer my call. People working in his facility believe tries to harass him as his ex-wife. I told them there is a case and hope the social workers convince Richard to fight for his money. They don't care.

I already set an appointment with a lawyer today. I told Richard, but he doesn't show up.

Lewis

I can't help you with anything.

Pia

Your grandfather mentioned you in his will. He knew your father is sick and never pay child support. The Fishman family owes me money. It is imposable that he gave all his money to people who have no blood relationship with him. I still remember how happy he was when you were born. It is imposable that he not gives you a penny when he died and can no longer enjoy his money. Can you go to the lawyer's appointment and file the case to challenge that will?

Lewis

It just so happens that I have a day off today. OK, I will help you get some child support back. that is, it.

Angel talks to Sydney

Look. This is also my arrangement, let Lewis have a day off that day. Otherwise, Pia will cancel that appointment and let the probate will go. Actually, by law, Lewis has no right to object the will because his father is still alive. However, this is the only way for us to continue the case. You will see what happens?

Ext. Pia and Lewis in the law office of Hai.

Pia

We are going to challenge a will probate in court. The son of the testator, Richard Fishman, is absent today because he is mentally ill. Does the testator's grandson Lewis Fishman have a right to challenge the will?

Hai

I just won a case and helped a grandson to get some inheritance from his grandfather. Challenge will should be a Grandsons' right as well. But does Sydney have another son who might be interested to open the case?

Pia

He has an older son. I have his phone number.

Hai

Okay. Let me contact him.

After a while, Hai comes back.

Hai

Kenny told me to contact his lawyer, and his lawyer said he was very interested about that.

Pia

That is good.

The phone rings again. Hai picks it up.

Hai

Yes, it's me. I just talked to you.

Kenny's lawyer

I am sorry. Kenny just changed his mind. He said, "Let that will go." I don't understand; he was so excited ten minutes ago. Now he changes mind.

Sydney's spirit and the angel are around.

Angel talks to Sydney

I am the one who made Kenny give up. You will see things are complicated. His involvement will make things more difficult. He lives far and doesn't know the situation here. If he files the case, he will be the person who makes up the decision and messes up the whole thing.

Ext. In the courtroom. The court calls the case number. Palmer and her lawyer, Curtain, are looking around and don't respond until they see Pia's lawyer, Hai, approach the judge. They are disappointed that someone appeared in court to challenge their will.

Hai

I am representing Lewis Fishman, grandson of the deceased Sydney Fishman, to object the probate will.

Court

As I see, the testators have two sons. What are their opinions? Are they still alive? By law grandson cannot challenge a will, only when their fathers are pass away.

Hai

We don't know the older son's opinion. Lewis is the son of Richard, Sydney's younger son. Richard has mental problems. He collapsed when he knew his father left nothing to him. It is strange that as a Jew, he handled his ten- million-dollar asset like that.

Court

We still need the son to make the objection. I will give you two weeks to have his signature, or the will should be released in this court by then.

Ext. Outside the courtroom: Pia; Pia's Chinese lawyer, Hai; and an American lawyer. Hai turns to Pia.

Hai

This is Done. I invited him as my partner to handle this case. I will pay him from the fee you pay me and not cost you extra money. You have paid me ten thousand dollars already.

Pia looks surprised and says nothing.

Ext. Pia talks to her sister on the phone.

Pia

Lewis has no right to challenge the will. Only Richard can do it.

Richard still refuses to answer my calls.

Yin

This is a crucial moment. If I, were you, I will go to see him? You can't just solve problem by phone calls. Maybe he will change mind when he sees you travel two hours and personally show up there.

Angel talks to Sydney

I am the one sends a signal to Pia's sister to say so.

Ext. In the lobby of an adult home where Richard lives. Pia is waiting there.

A Paging Announcer

Richard Fishman, please come to the lobby; you have a visitor. Pia is still sitting there, watching the clock, walking back and forth. She was not allowed to get up to Richard's room. She doesn't know if Richard will come down to see him. She is writing a note.

Voice from the movie

Richard: Hope everything is fine for you. I have already paid ten thousand dollars legal fee. This is the last chance for us to claim your father's money. The court gives you two weeks to file the case. For the ten thousand dollars I paid you should at least do something. If you don't like to continue, you can simply withdraw it any time. You told me you want the money since you were three years old. Your mother fought all her life for that because you deserve it. You can't give up like that

Pia
(talking to herself)

It is so difficult to deal with a retard and crazy guy. Enough is enough!

Pia walks out of the building. She drinks the soup that she prepared for Richard and acts like she is drinking a cup of bitter wine.

Ext. When Pia walks out of the building, Richard shows up at the lobby. He is upset, sick, and confused. He looks around. In the front desk he reading Pia's letter.

Ext. The American lawyer, Done, is sitting with Richard at the lobby after 15 minutes.

Richard

Were you sent by Pia?

Done

She is paying us, but she doesn't know I am here to see you. I can also represent you if you signed the agreement and pay contingency. This is a special offer to you. You don't need to pay a penny until you get the money. No lawyer charges this way for this kind of case.

Richard

Here it is! (Richard signs a document and pushes it back to Done.) I might withdraw the case anytime if you consider that I am crazy.

Ext. Pia and her sister Yin are on the phone.

Pia

Richard signed the paper, and we can file the objection now. But that day, I have another court case with a tenant. Our nephew, Seamon, insists that as the manager I must show up in the court room. Maybe I can just let the lawyers take care of the will. That is what we need a lawyer for.

Yin

I am also Seamon's aunt. I will go to the rental court for you. You know that I hardly help you even if you beg me. I believe the will case is more important at this moment. That is why I give you a hand. You will regret if you don't show up there.

Anger are around and talk to Sydney's spirit

I sent signal to Yin and make her involve, convince pia to the court for your will.

Ext. Pia, Hai, and Done are in the courtroom, as well as the will drafter, Curtain, and Diana.

Pia goes to the restroom on the fourth floor. From the stairs, she sees Done and Curtain are talking on the third floor. Hai is ten feet away from them. The whole picture looks suspicious.

Camera gets close to Curtain and Done.

Curtain

Congratulations. You finally filed the case. We were supposed to not see each other this way. But you told me you have an important message. What is that?

Done

I should congratulate you, as well. Our rejection will give you a good chance to make money.

Curtain

I will have no benefit in this lawsuit but troubles. I told them to hire some other lawyers for the case. I am not going to involve.

Done

Anyway, I think I have good news for you. I in charge of this case now for Richard has signed me an agreement. That means he will be under my control. If you promise to settle this case, I will let him pay by contingency. You know this kind of case usually end up with settlement.

Curtain

How much do you expect from the settlement?

Done

One hundred thousand dollars should be good for us. I will make Richard accept my proposal. He is an idiot who would consider ten a few ten thousand dollars as big money. To control him, we must get rid of his ex-wife. It is absolutely a good deal to spend one hundred thousand dollars for ten-million-dollar asset.

Ext. In Hai's office.

Done

I almost have a settlement with Palmer's lawyer. I ask for one hundred thousand dollars. We can give Richard twenty thousand dollars and keep the other as legal fee. For doing that we must get rid of Pia.

Hai

I have already signed an agreement with her.

Done

She has no right to sign any agreement, not even her son, Lewis Fishman. I have Richard's agreement on hand already. She has no choice but step down. For us, she must be out no matter what. How to talk to her is your problem. We can throw a big bill to her and force her to give up automatically.

Ext. Pia walks into Hai's office.

Hai

We can continue the case now but have to deal with Richard directly. We are very appreciative that you introduced this case to us. You will have your share according to the deal you made with Richard.

Pia

What do you mean? I am the one who pay the legal fee. We are always together even though we need him to submit the objection. He can't without me.

Hai

Don't worry. We allowed him to pay after he has the money.

Done
(talking to Pia)

Look at the response from the Palmers' lawyers. Look at these pictures with Richard holding guns. He sent these pictures to his father, and that is committing crimes. They will have the will drafter testify that his father left him nothing because of that. Fishman's family lost contact for over twenty years. Sydney considered the Palmers as his family members and gave them all his money even though their aunt had already died.

Look at this affidavit on April 26. The will drafter Curtain also swore that Sydney's health condition was good enough to make a will. You are hopeless because you have no way to prove how Sydney thought. This kind of case usually is ended by settlement.

Hai

We are in a very disadvantaged situation. By law, a father can give his children nothing and leave the money to a cat as long as he put his wish down into a will. We don't have any information to challenge the will they probate. However, we are still asking them to prove that the man holding guns in the picture is Richard.

Pia

That is Richard. He lost his mind then, and to stop him, his father did call the policemen. I even went to the court with him. His father also hired a lawyer to defend him and made sure he not being charged in the court. His father knew that he was sick. We can base on that to fight back. Law will never punish people who are mentally ill, even killers are excused. It is stupid to ask them to prove that the man on the picture was Richard. If they prove that, we will have nothing to say.

Done

You are not our client anymore. You have no right to tell us what to do.

Pia

I am the one who pays the legal fee. I just paid ten thousand dollars to you.

Done

That is nothing, and the money was used up already. This is the new bill. You want to talk to me? Pay this first!

Ext. The bill shows $15,000. Pia reviews it.

Pia

We were in the courtroom for less than an hour that day, and you were even late. How can you charge eight hours' legal fee on that day?

Done

After that, we did research in the courtroom for this case.

Pia

That day we even don't know if we can have Richard's signature and start the case. No one will do research before that. It's dangerous to have you as our lawyer.

Done

I am sorry. It is too late for you to say so. You are nobody for us. You must step down.

Ext. Pia is on phone with Richard.

Pia

Richard, did you sign an agreement with Done?

Richard

Yes. That day you came first but I couldn't see you when I went down to the lobby. Done just shown up then and I thought you were together. That is why I signed the agreement. He is hired by you. No?

Pia

He is dangerous to us. No lawyer accepts contingency for this kind of case. I saw him talk to Curtain in the courtroom. It seems he had a settlement with Palmer. They will get rid of you with a little bit of money. They get most of the settlement fee and let Palmar keep all your father's money.

Richard

Let the lawyers take care of that. They should know what to do. Do you think you are smarter than lawyers?

Pia

They are smarter but greedy. Do you remember how those lawyers took your mother's money all these years? They made her pay even though they knew the Mexican divorce agreement was accepted in New York court already. Remember that: your mother's lawyer convinced you to take the custodian money from your father, he then kept all the thirty thousand dollars, and gave you nothing?

Richard says nothing and hangs up the phone.

Ext. Next morning. in Pia's apartment: Pia and Lewis. Pia is going to leave home for work. (Sydney and Angel are around. They touch Lewis and make him ask Pia.)

Lewis

How is everything? How is Richard?

Pia

He answered my call but refused to change lawyers. Those lawyers sent me a $15,000 bill tell me pay that first before talking to them.

Lewis

You paid $10,000 that day when he accepted the case. I was there with you.

Pia

They said that $10,000 have already used up. If Richard insists to hire them, I have no choice. They will cheat Richard to accept settlement and keep most of the money as legal fee. It is interesting! You are never concerned and ask about Richard. Okay, let me call him one more time.

Pia dials numbers on the phone, and hear Richard answered from the other side.

Richard

What do you want me to do? You want me to come over to Flushing? I can come now.

Ext. At a lawyer's office. Pia and Richard sit in the waiting area.

Pia

Richard, thanks for your cooperation. Please be patient. Lawyer is in court now. He will sure come back to the office today. I knew him for many years and he might not remember me. When I was at a difficult time, he did give me a hand. We have no time to shop around for a better lawyer. At least he will not double cross us. His name is Richard Allen Chan.

Angel talks to Sydney

I am the one makes Yin convince Pia got go to the court and over there she found out they are double crossing by those lawyers

Richard

I just don't want you to say I am mentally ill. If you, do it, I will withdraw the case. I know the court might assign a guardian for mentally ill patient. There is no point that I get the money but was sent a mental hospital by my guardian. That is what my father did when he became the guardian as his first wife.

Ext. Lawyer Chan walks in.

Chan

I am sorry to make you guys wait. How can I help you?

Pia

His father had ten million dollars assets and the probated will leaves his family nothing. All the money goes to the in- law of his third wife who died before him. We have lawyers to take care of this case, but I don't think they are honest. It looks like they double-crossed us.

Chan

Richard, you just sign the agreement with me, and I will take the case back and see what the problem is.

Ext. Two days later in Chan's office

Chan

They have passed all documents to me. I read them and already know how to start the case. By law, any will must attach with witnesses' affidavits, and they don't have it. Also, any will be involving donation must file to the government, and they didn't do it as well. This will have three donations, $500 each, two for New York City College and one for a church. No matter how much the donation is, they must submit that to the attorney general. Looks like we can start from here.

Charter 8

FORGERY, PERJURY UNDUE INFLUENCE AND DURESS

Ext. At Curtain's office: Palmer and Curtain.

Curtain

It is too bad! It is not as what we expected; no objector shows up at all. I can't believe that it is the crazy son challenge us not the professor son. Now we get caught. I don't want to be the lawyer of this case. You must hire one or two lawyers to defend for us. I have already made an affidavit for you. It is lucky that they have no evidence and witnesses to challenge my sworn. They must hope to get some clue about the provisions. If we answered questions carefully, they can't beat us.

Palmer

I will say I didn't know there was such a will till I found it at Sydney's draw. I didn't show up in the law office on the day when he altered the will.

Curtain

Still, you cannot explain why he treated his nieces-in-law that well. If you can prove that he fell in love with you, it will made sense that he gave you all his money. But in this case your guys distributed his money about evenly and you can't even proof how often you see each other.

Palmer

We have to distribute his money this way because all of us know that he gave us nothing when Aunt died. They wouldn't allow me to have his money alone.

Curtain

The instrument you handed it to me is your final agreement?

Palmer

It still has little bit different. Victor changed his mind at the last moment. He said Sydney loved him so much that forced our aunt give him all Sydney's inheriting. He can't stand that I got 40 percent and he only got 35 percent in the provisions.

Curtain

Olga got 20% and her name is listed in the front. Sydney's previous two will never mention such a name. Who is she?

Palmer

Our mother. We put her first to show our respecting. Her 20% actually was split from Victor's provision. When mother passed away, he will have it back. He said he do us favor already he can't stand my provision is high than him eventually. Since it is not easy to make the deposition instrument, I decided to just change the amount in the will. I think 5 percent off in the will should not be a problem.

Curtain

Small change might cause a big trouble, 5% of ten million dollars means half million dollars. You risk my reputation to make perjury for only two million dollars and you're sitting there, getting eight million dollars. I am stupid.

Palmer

You are retiring and reputation is no longer important for you. Okay. We paid the legal fee and tax. You get net cash for the two million dollars. Let us continue.

Ext. Sydney's spirit and the angel are watching their conversation.

Sydney's spirit

My family knows nothing about how I thought when I altered the wills. I must send some documents to help them. I will make the Palmers disclose my first will, second will, reason that I break up with Kenny, how I fought for visiting Kenny's children, and the medical report about my eyes.

Angel

What does your first will say?

Sydney

That is one year after Richard sent me those pictures with him holding the gun. I have no right to visit Kenny's children because I refused to end relationship with him. In that will I still gave Richard something because I knew he was sick and didn't really blame him. I donated 40 percent of my assets to two city colleges for appreciating they gave me education chance to become a CPA. I divided the other 60 percent to my grandchildren.

Angel

Did anybody know your deep feeling to Richard and your school?

Sydney

It seems Pia noticed that. She presents her argument. One year after I received those pictures, I didn't really get mad and still give Richard money. How can I still angry when Richard stops bother me for twenty years but I still punish him in my last will?

Angel

Do you know who is Richard? Do you know why you refused to abandon him in spite of losing contacts with Kenny's family.

Sydney

I don't understand why I made that choice neither. End up I lost all my family members. that means the struggles in my whole life have no any meaning. All my money now goes to those evils. When I think of that, when I see they laugh loudly my heart is broken.

Angel

Listen, Richard's previous life is your retard brother. He commits suicide to let you have more food. When he came back to be your son, Richard, he has some improve but still sick in some way.

Sydney

I remember, before five years old, I had a brother always gave me his food. He hardly talks but had feelings, smiling, and cried sometimes.

Ext. reshow Bessy is crying and holding a kid's body. People around her take the body away and say "He is already dead. We saw him walk toward the river. We thought he could swim, and we didn't know that he was struggling for a while and sank to the water.

Sydney's spirit crying

Oh, my poor brother, I still remembered how he look at me when I asked for more food. Oh, my poor Richard. He never knew how I love him as well.

Angel

You refused to abandon Richard, but you leave your children nothing in the second will. Why?

Sydney

It is Diana's undue influence over her aunt. They forced me to give Teresa 50 percent of my assets. My vision was getting worse and worse in those days. By law, Teresa had been married to me for over thirty years; as my wife, she was entitled to have something even though those are all my money.

Ext. Back to year of 2008, Sydney, Teresa, and Diana in their apartment.

Teresa

I have something talk to you about your will. It is nice that you let me handle your estate fund after you passed away. But when I die, all the money must go back to your family or go to the charity. That means as your wife, I don't have any control on that. It looks like you actually leave nothing to me and just let me hold those money for a while. You know I love my sister's family and I hope can pass something to them.

Sydney

Who made you think things this way? By law I have absolute right to arrange my assets that I accumulated alone all these years. Most of them are saved before I married you.

Teresa

We've been married for over thirty years. Some of those assets grow after we got married. As your wife, I deserve something. In case we divorce now, the court will give me something. No?

Sydney

All these years I paid all the family expenses include all the travel fees when we traveled all over the world. I let you keep all your salary; all my ex-wives were not that lucky like you.

Teresa

We are good company, aren't we? I made you happy, and they couldn't. They made your live-in hell. Now you can't see I still take care of you so well and I promise to do it for the rest of your life.

Sydney

Okay. I get your point, and I believe it is Diana unduly influencing you. You can own 50 percent of my assets, but when you pass away all my money must go to Victor, your nephew only. Nothing to Diana and only $5000 to each of her children. If they challenge my will, they will not get a penny. Only you can probate my will, not anybody else.

Ext In front of a desk, Sydney pulls out few papers with his letterhead, writes down his intentions, and puts a stamp at the end. He was very unhappy and hands the paper to Teresa.

Sydney

Dianna undue influence you and your duress me. I can't see I have no choice. You contact Curtain. When it is ready, I go sign it.

Ext. At Curtain's law office. Teresa walks in. Curtain's secretary is typing the Will.

Secretary

The will should be ready soon.

Teresa's shows up for read by Sydney's will alter, disturbing the secretary's thinking. She types "her" instead of "him" in the will.

Movie's voice. "Testator, in our presence, subscribed and sealed the foregoing instrument and declared the same to be her last will and testament; and we, thereupon, at her request and in her presence and in the presence of each other, have hereunto subscribed our names as attesting witnesses."

Voice of the Film

This paragraph was copied to the probated will eight years after and was signed by the witnesses. It means in the will processing, what they see is a woman, her, but not a man, he, to sign the will. Actually, that huge error is enough to make the will invalid but the judge let it go.

Ext. Go back to Sydney and Angel.

Sydney's spirit

Diana unduly influenced her aunt to take over 50 percent of my assets. I, meanwhile, had to keep the donations as I promise to God. I had no choice but to put my family away. Now they use that as an excuse to say I don't love my family. I worked so hard all my life and made my family suffer so much. Still, we got nothing. If I can make the choice again, I will not send Kenny's mother to a mental hospital. I will not use the Mexico divorce to drive Gladys crazy. I didn't know that for these ten million dollars, my life would end up so ugly.

Angel

It looks like this case involved all the crimes: forgery, perjury, undue influence, and duress. You are blaming us for the sufferings we arranged for your family. However, we still don't know what will happen. It depends on whether Pia fights to the end and if some lawmakers legalize the crimes Palmer and Curtain committed. Pia has already spent one-hundred thousand dollars on legal fees. She had nobody support her not even her son. She can only with Richard, a retard guy. The problem is she know nothing about how you actually think. We will let Palmer provide some useful document to her.

Ext. At Palmer's lawyer's office, beside Palmer and Curtain, there are two lawyers, Messina and Haas. Sydney's spirit and the angel are hanging out around them.

Diana Palmer

Can we not send the first will and the second will to them? They don't know there are such documents at all, and we can just say that the probate will is the only will he made. His children could not deny the fact that the family didn't contact each other for twenty years. It makes sense that he considered us his family. Only one will can make things much simple.

Sydney and the angel are standing next to Haas and make him say.

Haas

By law, we must forward all the document we have to them. It is too late to hide those wills. Remember, in Curtain's affidavit, he mentioned that he drafted three wills for Sydney, plus his wife's will. That affidavit has been sent out in April.

Messina

The second will made it so clear that he will give nothing to his children because they refused to see him. He had stamped on his handwritten note, and nobody will doubt that is not his intention. Since that will give 50% of his asset to his lovely wife. So, it makes sense that when his wife passed away, he forwards those money to her family.

Curtain

Have my strong sworn back up, nobody will doubt the provisions on the probated will is forgery.

Diana Palmer

Okay. We can release those two wills to them. But we should not release the case that he fought for visiting the children of Kenney. Because those proofs he had strong affection to them. I don't think we need to request those records from the court. I beg Richard knows nothing about that and Kenney will not disclose why he didn't contact his father all these years.

Ext. Sydney's spirit sends a signal to Haas, the movie screen showing typed words: "You can make a lot more legal fee when you request, review, and make arguments for those documents."

Haas

Requesting those records just costs one hundred dollars as fee. Having that, we can know clearly about the family's relationship. We need to make some preparation in case they have arguments about that.

Diana Palmer

If it just cost a few hundred dollars, go ahead to request for it. But do we need the doctor's note? How his vision was should be their concern, not ours? We knew his health condition and we must say he can read.

Messina

We still need to know what the doctor said about his health condition. If something they listed is not good for setting a will, we have prepared how to answer for that. Also, to make the will more trustworthy, we should insist that the beneficiaries never know and never involved in the will sign. Diana found the Will in the drawer after he died.

Diana Palmer

It seems your guys know what to do. Just go ahead to do it. I believe we will be Okay, because I will have six affidavits from his neighbor, his CPA, and his cousin, proof that his mind was clear enough to set a will and he didn't like Richard.

Chapter 9
DEPOSITION

Ext. In the law office of Chan, Sitting: Pia, Richard, and Mr. Chan.

Chan

Look, this is Sydney's medical report they requested. You worry that his condition is good enough to set up a will. It said Sydney was legally blind when he signed the will. This is an important information for us. However, legally blind has different degrees. Some people still can read with magnify glass. This report is not strong enough for us to reject that probate will.

Pia

It is interesting that in Curtain's affidavit he didn't mention Sydney's vision problem at all. Up to April 2016 they still tried to hinder something.

Chan

96 years old and blind Sydney need someone took him to the office that day. We need to contact that person and see if can get information from there.

Ext. In a room: Mr. Chan, Diana, Haas and Messina and the typewriter for the deposition. The court reporter asks Diana to put her hand on the Bible and swear an oath.

Reporter

Please remember everything you say in this deposition will be just as if you are testifying in court in front of a judge.

Diana

(raising her hand)

I swear that everything I answer in this deposition is truth.

Chan

When was the first time you met Mr. Curtain?

Diana

In the will-signing day. (Diana think of the day she took Sydney to Curtain's office. They shake hands and then Curtain told her wait in the living room.

Chan

Do you mean the date of September 6, 2016?

Diana Palmer

Wait for a minute! The first time I met Mr. Curtain was on the will-reading day, not on the will-signing day. I might be in New York that day, but I never involved the willsigned. I didn't know there was such a will signed until I found it in Sydney's drawer.

Chan

Did Sydney ever mention his will to you guys before he died?

Diana Palmer

No, none of the beneficiaries knew that he gave us all his assets. As a matter of a fact, we were surprised for what he did.

Chan

You mean you guys even didn't have a chance to appreciation him for the ten million dollars he gave you. Those assets he accumulated in all his life.

Haas

Objection. It is not the moment to make a personal comment.

Chan

Mrs. Palmer, may I ask you the beneficiaries in the will you probated? From the last name, we can see that they are all your family member except Ana M. Garzon. Who is she?

Diana Palmer

She is the daughter of Teresa's brother in Ecuador. She is my cousin, but I never met her in the past fifty years until she had a trip to New York when our aunt had cancer.

Chan

That means you don't consider she is a close family member for you.

Diana Palmer

No, I don't. We never contacted each other in our life.

Chan

Do you think it make sense that Sydney considered she was his family member?

Haas

Reject for the comment.

Chan

Okay, let us talk about the first name in the will, Olga Palmer. Who is she? This name was never mentioned in the previous two wills. But in the last Will she is the first beneficiary.

Diana Palmer

Olga is my mother, Teresa's younger sister. Olga helped Teresa immigrate to the United States and totally changed Teresa's life. Teresa believed she owes my mother a big favor, and she considered we are her children. She did plan to give all her money to us.

Chan

If Teresa did not die before Sydney, you might keep that wish. Did Olga have any special relationship with Sydney, such as affair?

Diana Palmer

No, not at all. Sydney is my mother's brother-in-law.

Chan

Did Sydney ever stay overnight in your home? Did your mother ever have a trip with them together?

Diana Palmer

Not at all. We live in NJ. They live in New York. We only met each other in the big holidays. They went back to New York the same night.

Chan

That means every year you just meet each other a few times in the big holiday. Sydney never mentioned Olga in his first two wills. How come he put her as the first beneficiary in the probated will? Sounded like she was the most important person out of all the Palmers. Are you the people who made the will and put your respective mother in the first?

Haas

Objection! Counsel should not make an accusation like that.

Chan

In the probated will, Sydney put down how his money goes if beneficiaries predecease him. Those terms were never mentioned in his previous wills as well. It is unusual that a ninety-six-year- old man had that kind of worry. Do you know the reason?

Diana Palmer

I don't know the reason. Maybe because Teresa died all of a sudden, that made him believe that anything could happen. He cared about our benefits.

Chan

That will look more like you guys are making up a will to distribute his assets and it discloses your worry.

Haas

Counsel has no right to declare his opinion in here.

Chan

Okay, tell us about Victor. Where does he live now? Are you seeing each other often? In the will, you live in the same address.

Diana

No, he lives in Hawaii. Since he graduated from college, he never lives at home. He hardly contacts us. I didn't talk to him for almost ten years until recently. We don't get along.

Chan

How about Cynthia? Does she live in the same address the will list?

Diana

No, she lives in South Carolina. She came up to New York once or twice a year to visit our mother. Her son is autistic, who always screams in a closed place such as the airplane. Every time she came to New York she rushes to go home.

Chan

It looks like you don't have close relationship and hardly contact each other in the last twenty years. How can Sydney feel warm in such family and embrace you as his family members? In this probated will he gave each of you one million dollars up, including the one in overseas that he never met. For such a big grief he even didn't that expect appreciation from your guys. Does it make sense?

Haas

Objection, Mr. Chan is misleading my client. We don't need his comment on the relationship between Palmer's family and the tester at this moment.

Diana

I don't know how he thought neither. I just saw what were listed in his will. I so hope can appreciated him face-to-face. But we have admitted that anything could happen in the real life. The assume of "imposable" is not a proof. You must have witnessed or evident to proof the provision list in his will does not reflect his attention.

Chan

Last question. Did you ever see Sydney read?

Diana

He always carried a magnifying glass. I guess he could read.

Chan

Do you mean he could read typed words in the document?

Diana

(*pauses for a while*) Yes, he can read documents.

Court Reporter

Please remember that everything you say in this deposition will be same as when you are testifying in court in front of a judge.

Curtain

I swear that everything I said in this deposition is truth.

Chan

Mr. Curtain. Are you still practicing law?

Curtain

I should say no at this moment. I am very sick now.

Chan

Were you practicing law when you altered the will for Sydney?

Curtain

Yes. I made three wills for him, plus his wife's will.

Chan

Where was your office when you made the last will for him?

Curtain

I didn't have an office then. It was in my apartment, Manhattan, Seventy-Sixth Street. There are two rooms: one is my office room, and one is my bedroom. I was half-retired then. Sydney came to me because I am the one who prepared his previous wills.

Chan

Are you his lawyer who takes care of all his other business?

Curtain

No, I know nothing about his businesses. I even don't know how much assets he had until after he died. He only put percent on his will, and the dollars amount he mentioned is not over fifty thousand dollars.

Chan

How did you know him and when?

Curtain

I knew him thirty years ago. He saw my name in an ad p o s t e d in the street. I was a member of New York University law community then.

Chan

Can I conclude that you knew each other on the street? You don't have any intersection in his social life. You don't have a common social circle where people knew both you and him.

Curtain

You can say so. He kept everything in secret. That is why he brought in no witnesses when he signed the will. I had to find two witnesses for him. My wife and my neighbor.

Chan

How many times had he visited you for making his final will?

Curtain

Two times. The first time, he told me his intention. A few days after, when I got the paper ready, he came over to sign. He told me on phone that he needed to alter his will because his wife just passed away.

Chan

Do you remember how he came to your office? Such as is there anybody took him there?

Curtain

First time, he came with Ana, one of the beneficiaries. Both me and my wife remembered that very clearly because Ana introduced herself to us. She was living at his home and taking care of him.

Chan

How about the second time, when he came for signing the will?

Curtain

We didn't see Ana the second time. Must be a maid who took him to our office that day.

Chan

Can you describe the maid in a general way? Her skin color, her age?

Curtain

I am sorry I didn't pay attention to that. I was busy to greet Sydney.

Chan

Did Sydney walk into your apartment alone? He was blind. Theoretically, even though he didn't like anyone was around him. We need to contact someone who is not the insider.

Curtain

I am sorry. I really don't remember who took him into the office. I just remember no beneficiary in his will were show up that day.

Chan

How about your wife? She remembered Ana she must also have some memory about the maid who was waiting in your living room. Your wife usually greets the guesses. Doesn't she?

Curtain

I don't think she remembered, neither, and that is why we don't have any information about her.

Chan

Do you have a waiting area beside the living room?

Curtain

I should say no.

The maid must step out apartment and wait in thehallway.

Chan

Can Diana provide us the contact information about the maid they hired for Sydney in those days?

Curtain

I am afraid she didn't know neither. She lives in NJ. Most things were taken care of by her auntie and Ana.

Chan

So, Ana must know that. All the time, she was around to take care of everything for Sydney. Why was she absent that day?

Curtain

I am afraid she didn't know neither. Sydney had the right to tell her "Don't go with him "and get someone else as company.

Chan

If he loved the Palmer family that much and even gave them all his money, why had he kept them away like that when he alters the will? He should let them know his intentions ahead and celebrated it together, gotten some appreciation from them, at least.

Curtain

That I don't know. I hardly know how he thought.

Chan

But you swore in your affidavit that Mr. Fishman "provided for his residuary estate to be distributed amounts members of his deceased wife's family, whom he had come to embrace as his own family." The last sentence is your construction or he told you face-to-face directly.

Curtain

Those are my words. That day, he handed me the instrument and told me to base on the number on it to distribute his assets. It is all for the Palmers, and that is why I believed he loved them.

Chan

Did he ever mention his affection to them in front of you?

Curtain

No.

Chan

You put it as a sworn in your affidavit. As his will drafter, you actually created his motivation for this probated will. Let us go back to the instrument. What did he say when he handed that to you?

Curtain

He said "Please base on this number to alter my will."

Chan

Did you have any video or audio tape to back up the process and record what he said?

Curtain

No. But he is the only one who handed that to me orally. I didn't expect he did that, and that is why I didn't prepare equipment to record it.

Chan

Do you have witnessed? What I mean it was there anybody around when he handed that in to you?

Curtain

No.

Chan

No? Not even your wife, who was the witness and lives in your apartment.

Curtain

No, not even my wife. She was presented when Sydney got ready to sign the will.

Chan

Did you read the will in front of your wife and the other witness?

Curtain

No. They didn't know any content of the will. I didn't read it in front of the witnesses. I sat side by side with Sydney and explained things to him. He read the paper with the magnifying glass. I don't know if he could read it, but he kept looking and looking that.

Chan

Let us discuss this instrument more. You can see the signature on that will, right? Sydney could hardly control his hand. How come the words in the instrument were arranged so well, the lines are straight. The words are identical and made by strong strokes. It didn't look like were written by a ninety-six-year-old man. I don't think I can write big characters that well. Can you do that and show us how well you can write?

Screen show the original instrument when Chan makes the comment.

Haas

Reject! Counsel can't make witness do anything here.

Chan

Did Sydney write this in front of you?

Curtain

No. But he was the only one who handed that paper to me.

Chan

Just as what you emphasize in your affidavit that "all of the substantive changes were provided to me by Sydney H. Fishman, and by him alone," it looked like you hoped to convince us that no one was involved, such as making it in a computer by copy and paste.

Haas

Object. Consult can't make assumption without proof.

Chan

Besides this, did Sydney submit other papers to support his will? This instrument didn't mention anything about will, not $ sign, no % sign. Those numbers can mean apples or coins. Also, that instrument has no stamp or signature like the note he submitted in the second will.

Curtain

I don't know how he made the instrument; I know he told me that basing on those numbers to prepare the provisions of his new will.

Chan

Let us make further discussion. Why the provision in the will is different from this instrument. Diana's share was changed from 40 percent to 35 percent in the will. That difference actually involves with half a million dollars. As a will drafter, how come you alter the number and against your client's wish?

Curtain

No! No! I guess he told me to make the update from the phone after he left the office.

Chan

As a lawyer, you must have the record on your phone. Right?

Curtain

I am sorry I don't have that.

Chan

That means you have no supports, no witnesses, no video or audio record for this key instrument. You only present your sworn. Did he submit any information to support his will besides that instrument?

Curtain

I guess no. But I had the instrument with provisions he wrote down. The probate will be based on that. We have some scratching paper to show how the probated will was composed.

Chan

Again, those scratching papers don't have witnesses or video to back up. You can do it later and write whatever you want to wright. Okay, you said no other information he submitted to you and no any beneficiaries involved in the will alerting. Who told you to put down in case the beneficiary predeceases Sydney how their money goes? Is that Sydney's idea? Why he didn't have that worry in the last two wills. Are the beneficiaries themselves told you to put that down?

Curtain

I don't remember how that were composed. All the beneficiaries were mentioned in the previous will, and I just kept their information and update the provision.

Chan

I am sorry, Mr. Curtain. We reviewed very carefully. Sydney never made that kind of arrangement in his first two wills.

Curtain

Maybe Teresa dying suddenly made him have that kind of worry.

Chan

How did he convey that kind of message to you? And when?

Curtain

I guess on phone.

Chan

You guess? But that instruments didn't say anything besides numbers. Let me ask you one more question. (Chan looks at a piece of paper and reads.) In the probated will, it lists Ana Garzon residing in: Francisco Oliva Oe3-73 yCap Edmundo Chiriboga Case #46, Quito, Ecuador. Who gave you this address? It should not be Ana because as what you said no beneficiary involved the will alert. Now the question created: can a ninety-six-year-old blind man memorize such a long address and forward that to you? You are at your sixties; can you remember it and repeat it to me?

Curtain

I can't. I can't do it, and I don't remember how I got the information neither. Is it from the previous will?

Chan

Ana was never mentioned in the first two wills at all. Also, regarding the donations. In both the first two wills, Sydney gave 40 to 50 percent of his assets to two city colleges and one religion organization. It is about four to five million dollars. In your probate will, the amount was changed to 1500 dollars. How did Sydney indicate to you about his huge change? What did he say exactly?

Curtain

He didn't say too much on that. He just told me to adjust the provision according to that instrument. Because he gave 100 percent to the Palmer family, which means his donation will drop to zero, and I therefore put down $500 to each of them.

Chan

How did Sydney mention Lewis? Lewis was the only Fishman family member in the second will as a direct beneficiary. In your scratch paper, you put Lewis's name next to Kenny's children and said they refused to see their grandfather. That obviously was not truth. Pia kept sending Lewis's information to Sydney, including Lewis's handwritten letter. It made no sense that before he died, Sydney still slandered grandson for giving out his money to people who share no blood with him.

Curtain

I, I, I didn't remember. I put his name there must have been some reason.

Chan

In your affidavit you said, "All of the substantive changes were provided to me by Sydney H. Fishman and by him alone." What was not changed in the October 6, 2014, will was the following provision.... words you typed to attack Richard are exactly as same as the will 8 years ago. Did Sydney say that to you again on the day he set up his last will? Or you just copied it from the previous will?

Curtain

I copied it from the previous will.

Chan

That means you don't have any document or recorder to prove what Sydney's exact thinking about Richard when he altered his last will. You just copied what he wrote eight years ago and proved that he still hates Richard even though Richard did not bother him for over twenty years.

Curtain

They didn't see each other again; means they still don't like each other.

Chan

Mr. Curtain, the probated will was only based on an instrument that had no testator's signature or stamp. It mentioned nothing about will provision. It had no support by witnesses, video, and audio tapes. All claims are relying on your sworn. For a ten- million- dollar testament, do you think the supports you provided are enough?

Haas

Objection, counsel has no right to make conclusion. He is misleading my witness.

Ext. Deposition for Curtain's wife, Halen.

Chan

As a witness, did you know the provision of Sydney's will?

Halen

No. I know nothing about that. I think Mr. Curtain explained that to him side by side. When they were ready, he called the witness to show up and watch Sydney sign.

Chan

Did Curtain read the will loudly in front of all of you, the witnesses and Sydney? Did you hear Sydney say "Yes, that is my will?"

Halen

I don't remember what happened exactly. I just know Curtain did take time to explain the will to him because—

Chan

Curtain did it. Is it because Sydney could not read?

Halen

I don't know exactly about that, but I remember I saw a magnifying glass.

Chan sneers.

Chan

Do you mean you see Sydney read the will with a magnifying glass?

Halen

I have bad memory. I saw someone read something with a magnifying glass. I am not sure if that is Mr. Fishman.

Chan

You're not sure? How many old men were in your apartment that day? You mentioned the magnifying glass and misled people that Sydney could read. You, meanwhile, refused to testify that you saw Sydney use a magnifying glass to read his will because you knew he could not read a typed document even with a magnifying glass. You don't want to make perjury unless you have to.

Haas

Objection. Counsel has no right to make conclusion.

Ext. In Haas's office were Palmer, Curtain, Haas, and Messina.

Curtain

I am collapsing. Their question is so sharp. You put me into the front to block all the bullets. I can't hold it anymore. If there is further hearing, I will not cooperate. I have to withdraw my affidavit.

Palmer

We can't explain why he leaves all his asset to five of us. Why he even withdrew the donations that he kept for twenty years.

Curtain

Don't consider that I am your only gun. You can use the other witnesses' affidavits, his neighbor, his cousin, his CPA, and all the people you can find.

Palmer

All those witnesses can just mention about his health and the relationship between him and Richard. They couldn't explain why he changed his will a lot and gave all his assets to us. As the will drafter, you are the right person to confirm his intention. Judge will take your words.

Curtain

If you admit that you took him to sign the will and you also provide information to him for alter the will, I don't have to answer all those questions. You took the money and refuse to make any involvement. It is not worth to take those risks and make those money.

Palmer

Those are a lot of money; you can make it all your life. You must do something.

Curtain

You can use my sworn to convince the judge but I have to withdraw that in the last moment, the court hearing. Hope the judge already took our point. If she gives us the money, I will have my share. If she finds out what we did, all of us must take the responsibility, not just me.

Palmer

Okay. That is the deal. You will get two million dollars. See if we are lucky enough to win the case.

Chapter 10

OBTAIN STRONG EVIDENT

Ext. In Chan's office: Chan, Pia, and Richard. Sydney's spirit and the angel are around.

Chan

Many of their words are suspicious and contradictory. But they can say that is what we believe. We have no witnesses or documents to proof that they committed perjury and forgery.

Pia

Look at this initial, (*Pia show a paper with an initial*)

They can change the will by substituting the page where listed the provisions. They still have Sydney's original signature at the last page. I think the initial in that provision paper looked weird. I sent that to a handwriting expert and I got an answer from him yesterday.

Chan

What did he say? Is him a qualify handwriting expert?

Pia

He compares with Sydney's other initials and said the one in the provision paper is forgery. He has a school teach how exam hand writings. He attaches all his certificate and list all his background with a serious notary.

Chan

That is the first professional document we summit to them and it is very important. How about we summon all the other beneficiaries, Victor and Ana, Olga? It needs to get the approvals from the court first.

Pia

They are from the same group. They will protect each other desperately. I am not interested in dealing with them. I prefer to get help from Vanguard, his bank. I hope as the third party they can provide some useful information to us honest.

Chan

Vanguard is in Philadelphia. It will be very expenses if we go there with a whole team for the deposition. It might need more than ten thousand dollars.

Pia

I don't mind paying that. Besides the bank, no one will help us. We don't have the maid. We can't picture the whole situation. From the information theyprovide,Sydney refused to end contact with Richard, and end up he could not see Kenny's family anymore. That means in the depths of his mind, Sydney never really blamed on Richard.

Chan

We have the letter from the attorney general of the State of New York. Lisa Barbieri, assistant attorney general, believes that "Palmers and someone acting independently involve duress, undue influence, forgery, and perjury. That paper will they probated was not duly executed. Sydney Fishman was not competent to make a will."

Pia

She listed all the possible crimes in her letter, and it seems everything she accused is correct now. But attorney general of State of New York doesn't involve anymore for the donation is not bid enough.

Chan

Okay, I will request the information from the broker Jeffry in Vanguard and see how they respond.

Ext. In an office of Vanguard: a whole team is working; they pick up all tapes recording the telephone conversation between Sydney and Jeffry. They pull out all the documents Sydney and Diana signed.

The Lawyer from Vanguard

I will send the document in the name of Vanguard's legal team but no in the name of Jeffry. Jeffry makes no comment or swear about this case. He just talked on phone with Sydney, and the conversation was recorded well in the tapes. The phone record covers everything. It self is a strong proof.

Ext. In Haas's office: Diana Palmer, Curtain, Haas, and Messina.

Haas

Oh my god! They forwarded us the flash drive provided by Vanguard.

It recorded all conversation between Sydney and the broker Kern. Sydney's word hit us good......

Meanwhile, the movie displays the scene Sydney tale with Jeffry on phones again about he can't read any words typed on paper A magnifying glass can only help him read large printed words.

Massina

That put us in as very bad situation. For a blind man the law required the will drafter read his will loudly infront of the witnesses. Without that the process can't consider duly. Curtain already said that his witnessed didn't know the content of the will because he never read it infront of them.

Diana Palmer

It looks like we must insist say that Sydney could read with a magnetite glass.

The movie meanwhile displays the phone conversation about how Sydney was worry when Juffry told him to get help from his lawyer to fill out the forms. It shown he didn't trust Danna as well. He preferred to travel from Philadelphia to New York for the fund transfer.

Diana

He is a slippery fox. Every time he asked to help him, he acted like he trusted me very. Now he stabs me behind my back. What can we do? Can we make the flash drive invalid?

Haas

We can try our best. Look at this! Richard sent us 35 mails in the last five days. Those are notes written with very bid letter.

Ext. It show a lot of notes printed with big letter. and shows Richard is calling on phone. Curtain answered the phone in the other side and Richard hang up the phone.

Curtain

He calls me a few times and didn't say anything. I feel some kind of threatening.

Haas

We can use this as an excuse to stop their challenge. One of his mails said he is considering withdrawing the case because Pia and his lawyer want him to admit that he was mentally ill.

Ext. Pia is on phone, looking for Richard.

Operator

Richard doesn't want to answer your call.

Ext. in Chan's office Lawyer Chan and Pia.

Chan

Look at this letter. The other said they received twenty-two mails from Richard within just a few days.

The movie screen shows a paper with a large printed letter.

Chan

They said Richard harassed them. I read all the mails. He simply answered questions they issued in the deposition. For example, he said he did think of driving an airplane to hit his father's building because he loves his father so much and he was ignored. Those mails have nothing to do with harassment. I noticed that Richard was collapsing in the deposition. That is why I stopped them and arranged another deposition.

Pia

Richard refused to answer my call. We might lose him, and our case will be interrupted. It is important I want to pay you to visit him.

Chan

It will be expensive if I travel there to meet him. How about I write you a letter for free. You take a chance; he might change his mind and see you. I need his cooperation in urgent. Palmer has filed a letter ask for stopping this case for they felt threaten from Richard's schizophrenia.

Ext. In Richard's adult-home reception. Pia and Richard are sitting in the lobby.

Richard

I wrote a lot of letters to them. I just cannot help to do it. I think I messed up the case, I am sorry. I dare not face you. I know you have spent a lot of legal fees.

Pia

I have all the letters you sent them. If you want to continue, you go to see Mr. Chan with me now and make an affidavit.

Ext Pia and Richard are in Chan's office.

Chan

The court rejected their request and allow the case continued. Richard refuses to see a doctor and give us a note about his mental health status. Now they mention it. They finally admit. that.

Pia

Now we have some proof to submit: The only telephone tape records in this case, provided by Vanguard. Hand writing expert's affidavit and proof for Richard's mental health status.

Sydney's Spirit

I am the one who disturbed Richard and let them admit that he was crazy. They kept attacking Richard for harassing me but never mentioned the mental illness he has. Our law always has exemption to crazy people. it gives good advantage to this case.

Chapter 11
COURT HEARING AND JUDGE'S DECISION

Ext. In the courtroom for a court hearing. Lawyer Chan, Hass, Messina stand in front of the judge. Pia and Richard are sitting in the hearing benches. Diana Palmer and her husband are sitting on the other side. Sydney's spirit and the angel are hanging around, as well. The screen shows "Judges: Mella."

Chan

It is very important that testator Sydney Fishman was ninety- six years old and was legally blind when he altered his will. By law, a will drafter supposes read the will aloud, has witnessed watch the testator agreed with the will content and sign. However, the will drafter Curtain admit that he didn't have that procedure. Witnesses in this case therefore know nothing about the will.

Messina

Testator Sydney is just legally blind, which is a far cry from being actually blind. If you read Sydney's statement on Vanguard's phone recorder, he actually states that he can read with a magnifying glass. Will drafter Mr. Curtain have testified that he sat side by side with the decedent, reviewed provisions of the will? Sydney also used his magnifying glass to read the provisions.

Haas

Nothing provided as to the fact that testator couldn't read or he couldn't see.

Court Judge Mella

But the client does not dispute that the decedent didn't have perfect vision.

Haas

Right, we do not dispute that, Judge, but that doesn't mean that he could not fully and completely read and compare and execute his will. And the objectant hasn't presented anything in any viable form to show others.

Court Judge Mella

The fact that decedent had some visual impairment, even to the point of "legal" blindness, as objectant argues, does not change this conclusion because blind persons many make wills. Here, the attorney drafter testified that those dispositive provisions of the will were orally provided by the decedent shortly before execution.

Chan

Sydney had a telephone conversation recorded by Vanguard claimed that he could not read typed document. The instrument you mention with no witness, no video or audio tape backup. It only had the will drafter swear for it, and he didn't see the testator write it. That instrument doesn't not look like it was written by a ninety-six-year-old man who lost control of his hand and was blind.

The Court Judge Mella

The instrument was an actual will. It is clear enough to be the support. It doesn't need support anymore. The objectant doesn't have the product of undue influence, fraud, or duress. He has failed to demonstrate evidence against the probated bill.

Chan

We have a handwriting expert who reviewed the page with all the provisions listed. He concluded that the initial on it was fraud. They can easily change the provision by switching a paper.

Haas

That handwriting expert is not qualified to dismiss a will, and he didn't question the signature in the last page. As long as that signature is good, the will should be trustworthy.

The Court Judge Mella

Even if the court were to consider this letter an affidavit was an expert, there is no requirement that a testator initial the pages of a will for it to be valid, but concerns if the will has been signed at the end. That opinion letter does not address the real issue—whether it is the decedent's signature at the end of the will. Thus, the letter is insufficient to claim the will was not duly executed.

Messina

We have one more request here. The April 2016 was disclosed during discovery; however, counsel did not submit it in opposition to the motion for summary judgment but submitted it one day before oral argument. So based on that, we have not had an opportunity to respond to the April 2016 report. We ask that Your Honor reject the submission.

The Court

Well, most definitely that is not part of the record in the motion for summary judgment. So, did you want . . . ?

Haas

Very good, Judge.

Chan

May I just make one point on that, Your Honor?

The Court Judger Mella

I am sorry. Mr. Messina, were you done?

Messina

I just have one other point to address on counsel's points. He referred to the deposition. Sorry, the statement of the broker named Jeffry Kern. That statement was not admittance to form. It's not a testimonial statement it was not sworn to. Mr. Kern has not authenticated the statement. It was not submitted along with a business record certificate.

Chan

This is the only tape record in this case and it is provided by the legal team of Vanguard. Over there the decedent described his vision very clearly: he can't read, type words on paper. With a magnifying glass, he could only read large printed words.

The Court Judger Mella

That he could read or not is not an important issue. A blind man has the right to make a will. Here, the facts that an attesting witness could not confirm if the decedent had his magnifying glass that day, but the attorney drafter and one of the witnesses testified that he did.

Chan

We need the information of the aide who took Sydney to the will execution that day. They cannot even mention her skin color or age. All of them said they could not remember anything. We couldn't contact theaideat all. Maybe there was not such an aide. Beneficiary is actually involved in the will signed.

The Court Judger Mella

The testimony of the attorney drafter established that the beneficiaries had no direct involvement in the preparation or execution of the will. They said it was an aide who accompanied decedent to the will execution. They could not descript her because who appears to have stayed in a separate waiting area. Your argument is insufficient to rebut the presumption under the circumstances.

Chan

I hope you consider this, Your Honor: the objectant was suffering from being mentally ill all these years. He lost his mind when he sent out those letters or pictures to his father and messed up his family relationship. The family lost contact for over twenty years; that allowed many things to happen, unbelievable and unpredictable. This will be concerning ten million dollars. We should also make the beneficiary prove why they deserved all the money, including the five-million-dollar charity in the previous will. It is not appropriate to make decisions based on a forty- five-minute hearing.

In my opinion, just the errors on that will are enough to make it invalid. The document that the witnesses signed said that they saw Sydney Fishman "at her request and in her presence." The testator they saw was a woman. Also, the date of the affidavit was crossed out, and a current day was simply put in.

The Court Judger Mella

Those errors had nothing to do and are not enough to challenge the provisions of the will. The picture is very clear: the objectant admits that he never saw his father for the last nineteen years of his life. Moreover, objectant admits that over the years, he sent his father correspondence and photographs that were harassing or threatening. According to the attorney drafter's sworn, this was a natural will, benefitting members of the family of decedent's spouse, with whom decedent was close and whom he considered his family. He also swore that the decedent's mental faculties were intact and that it was the decedent alone in a meeting to tell him who will get his benefit and with what percentages.

In opposition, the objectant offered no evidence of unduly influenced decedent, duress, fraud, or perjury. No evidence of mistakes or misrepresentation, as well.

In examining all the evidence, the court determined that the will, on October 6, 2014, is valid and genuine and should be admitted to probate. Accordingly, the court granted the proponent's motion for summary judgment, and the objections to probate were dismissed.

The camera focuses on Pia, who is standing up and keeps waving to Chan, her lawyer.

The Court Judger Mella

Looks like your client keeps greeting you. I will give you a few minutes to find out what she wants to say.

Ext. Pia and Chan step out of the courtroom, and they see a few policemen holding guns there.

Chan

It is weird. I hardly see the court have so many policemen.

Pia

You have to emphasize that the will drafter never read the will aloud in front of the witnesses. Nobody knows what the decedent wants. For a blind man, the will process is not duly done.

Pia puts hands on the Chan's shoulder and encourages him. They walk into the courtroom again.

Chan

My client said the will was never read aloud in front of the witnesses. We all rely on what the will drafter said without requesting video or audio tapes back up.

The Court Judger Mella

We have already discussed this issue, the law concerning the capacity of the decedent towards the instrument. That instrument was an actual will. I will issue a decision explaining my reasoning, and that decision will be mailed to both sides.

Ext. Richard is angry and rushes out of the courtroom. Pia runs after him. Outside the courtroom, there are four policemen holding guns and stopping them.

Policeman

Please follow us when you go out of this building.

Pia

Why do you do that? We are not criminals.

Policeman

Correct, you are not criminals, but we were told that he is mentally disabled. We want to make sure things is under control in case he hears the court decision and loses his mind.

Pia

Good, you already have the decision before the hearing. You know his mental health statue and you don't give him an exemption. but don't mind to destroy him at the very beginning.

Pia has tears in her eyes. She holds hands with Richard when walking out of the building. She comforts Richard.

Pia

Richard, don't worry. Be calm; I will take care of you for the rest of your life.

Richard

I don't explode. I listen to you.

Ext. In Haas's office: Diana, Curtain, Haas, and Massina.

Haas

I don't expect that we can win so easily. She allows us to dismiss Curtain's key affidavit, and she still quotes most of its content, particularly Sydney's relationship with his nieces-in-law. Ha, ha, ha!

Curtain

You can't imagine how much pressure I have been taking. Thank God! I dismiss my affidavit in the hearing. This case is all base on the judge's decision, and it has nothing to do with me.

Massina

I can't imagine that she totally ignored the telephone records provided by Vanguard. Over there, Sydney did describe his vision clearly, he can't read words typed on the paper. I tried so hard to dismiss those records and I almost mess up the things. She simply ignored that. She also avoided mentioning Richard's mental problem. For us, she handled things perfect. We are over worry.

Diana

That is why I told you: you should not be afraid to take a chance. Now all of you make big money. All of us are happy, ten million dollars! That old man is very cheap. He used a tea bag twice, as well as a napkin. He waited for it to dry and reused it again. He saved all the money for the family of his lovely wife. Ha, ha, ha. His retard son wasted me so much legal fees, I will make them pay some back

Chapter 12
APPEAL

Sydney's spirit
That was how my money go! I don't believe things end up in this way. My family suffered so much, and I worked so hard. Pia has spent one hundred thousand dollars in legal fees. She will have no money to appeal. Will things stop here?

Angel
We will let Richard file the appeal. Pia writes the brief, and Richard corrects her grammar mistakes.

Ext. In the office of Surrogate's Court: Pia, Richard and the officers over there.

Pia
We need to appeal this case. We have no money to hire a lawyer. We will take care of it ourselves. Sydney altered a will at ninety-six years old and with blind eyes. Their witnesses knew nothing about the will and they just take over all Sydney's ten million dollars asset. His donations were deducted from five million dollars to fifteen hundred dollars.

Clerk
I heard this case. Yes, you can represent yourself.

Pia
We went to the New York State Appellate Division court.

A Ten Million $ Testament

They said the appeal must be submitted from here. Here is our brief.

Clerk

Correct. We can do it. But you have to attach it with an affidavit. *(Pia feels confused)* What is that for? We know nothing about the court procedure. Today is the last day to file it. Do we have time?

Clerk

You have to make a copy, send it to the other side, and attach an affidavit made by the person who sent the document. Here is the copy you can use. Fill everything out after your delivery the document and make a public notary. Not far from here, there is a copy center. You have to finish ASAP. We close at five o'clock. If you don't come back before that, your case is done, can't appeal any more.

Ext. Pia and Richard in a copy center. A clerk is nice enough to help them to make the copies.

Pia

We are lucky to have your help. Here is your tip.

Clerk

No. You don't need to pay for it. You have good luck.

Ext. In Hass's office. Pia hands the document to Hass, who refuses to take it.

Pia

You have no right to reject it. (She throws the thing at the desk.) Ext. In the store providing public notary Pia signing the affidavit

Pia

Can we just cross out the date and put another date in this kind of documents?

Clerk

No. affidavit with any update is considered invalid by law.

Pia

Thank you for such an important message.

Clerk

Everybody who takes the license must know such a basic thing.

Ext. In the office of Surrogate's Court, the clock points at four o'clock. Clerk puts things together and reviews a money order handed by Pia.

Clerk

You even run to the post office for a money order. It is amazing that you c a n finish all the process at the last minute. Now you go next door, submit everything at their window.

Pia

Thanks. (*Pia looks at Richard and shows him a relieved smile.*)

Ext. In Haas's office: Palmer and Haas.

Palmer

I thought we got rid of them already. I don't expect that they drop their appeal at the last minute. Can we say we didn't receive it before the dead line?

Haas

I can try to make an email and state that their appeal was sent after the expired day.

Curtain

My obligations to you are over. If we have to answer their appeals, you have to dismiss my deposition plus my affidavit in April 2016.

Haas

It is difficult to withdraw a deposition because that is same like you swear in front of the court. If you do so, we will lose all the supports for this will.

Curtain

Witnesses have the right to retract what they have sworn. That is better than committing perjury to all the end. I can't sleep every night now. I am stupid to torture myself and let the others get their money.

Ext. Richard and Pia are in the office of New York Appellate Division.

Clerk

Your case has been submitted to here. The file number is 2016-345. You can file your brief within six months. To get it ready, you need to put all your supported documents as a book in the magazine size. Your brief can't not be not more than fifty pages. You need to submit 10 set to us. Here is the sample.

The clerk knows they do the appeal the case by themselves and it involves ten million dollars; he shows sympathy. He hands in a few sample appeal copies related to Pia.

Ext. Pia finds out the format for starting the appeal. She prepares their brief according to the court's requirements. Types what she wants to say and has Richard correct it. She puts the document together, print that in a printing house then bind them into books. They have to run back and forth, put the books in a big box, move the box in and out of the subway stations and sent it to the court, New York Appellate Division.

Ext. It is in the morning, Richard is waiting outside a court building. Pia sees him from afar and runs to him.

Pia

Have you waited for a long time? It is only eight thirty.

Richard

I was here since seven thirty. I am afraid that I am late. I didn't have breakfast yet.

Pia

I know; I brought you a pancake I made this morning. We still have time; you can sit down and eat first. They tell us to come today, didn't say for what.

Ext. Richard sits and eats quickly. Food drops into his coat. Pia feels embarrassed for him. She stands in front of him and doesn't let the passers to see that.

Ext. In the courtroom. A fat woman looks like a man, very rude. She is the lawyer of the courtroom.

Woman

Who is Richard?

Richard

Me.

Woman

Are you appealing a case for your father's testament? You want to stop the court to release the money because you believe the case is in appealing? But the local court believes they deserve those money.

Richard

Those are my father's money. Someone who has no blood relationship with my father took all of his ten million dollars.

Haas

The judger believed the wills reflect your father's intentions. We must respect that.

Woman talks to Hass

You are the lawyer of Palmer Right? You and Richard come with me. We gave you a short argument hearing and then decided if this court accept the case. Both of you can get in but not you.

She turns to Pia and blocks her at the door.

Pia is shocked that this is such an important meeting and Richard has to handle it alone.

Pia

Richard is autistic. He doesn't know how to defend for himself.

Woman

You should know the law. You are not a lawyer; you can't represent him. If he appeals for himself, he is the only one can get into this room.

Ext. Inside a small courtroom. The court lawyer, Richard, and Haas. A clerk is typing and records their conversation.

Woman

Richard, you said they have no blood relationship with your father and take all his money. Do you know that your father had right to give his money to anybody as long as his will is valid?

Haas

That is how the judge in the lower court said. She believed Sydney didn't see his family for over twenty years proof that he considered the nieces of his third wife are his family. It is naturally that he gave them all his money.

Richard

They had no video or audio tape to prove my father's intention. Just a piece of paper that did not look like written by a ninety-six- year-old blind man.

Haas

But we also have his father's statement about Richard, it said: "I had him arrested and brought to court for harassment of me and my wife Teresa. I deliberately make no provision for him."

Woman Lawyer in the Court

Richard, is the statement truth?

Richard looks scared and embarrassed; he stops for a while.

Richard

That was twenty years ago; when I did that, I lost my mind. My father knew I was sick; to stop me, he called the policeman, but he also hired a lawyer to defend for me. I was not punished for that arrest. They even waived the court decision; I don't need to work in the community. I am wrong; I am sorry. I don't mean to harm my father. I love him very much. I just could not keep a job and had no income in those days. My father was rich. I thought after receiving those pictures, he will give me some money right away. I lost my mind; I am too stupid. I didn't do anything wrong for twenty years I don't think my father was still angry.

Richard starts to cry.

Haas

Your father also said that you hired a lawyer to sue him for money. That is why you receive no part of his estate.

Woman Lawyer

Is that truth?

Richard

It is truth. But that is my mother's lawyer, not hired by me. He came to me and asked if I wanted the custody money from my father. I said yes. That is the money my father saved for me when I was a kid. That lawyer stole those thirty thousand dollars my father paid and gave me not even a penny. Your lawyers took money from my mother, from me, and now they stole my father's money.

Haas talk to the woman lawyer

Richard has to take responsibility for what he did. He had no right to challenge the probate will.

Richard

I need more proof about my father's intentions before he died. Two years after I sent the pictures, he didn't really get mad and still left me some money in his first will. He could not visit Kenny's children and lost contact with all of his family because he refused to end contact with me. He knew I was sick he never really blames on me.

Haas

Sydney's statement was very clear, and Richard admitted that he once harassed his father. Feeling sorry now helps he go nowhere.

Richard

That probate will just quote the words my father said ten years ago, and without any backup document. The last time I called my father was after we lost contact for eighteen years. My father didn't hang up the phone; it seems he wanted to say something. We were silent for a while, and I am the one hung up the phone first because I was upset, but I could tell that he no longer hated me. He always told me that he works very hard for his family. It is impossible that he left all his money to those people. It is all my fault; I messed up things. *(Richard cries again.)*

Haas

That is what Richard said. He had no witness. We have the will drafter as the witness sworn that Sydney considered his wife's family as his family and intended to give them all his money. We have an instrument to list his wishes. The judge in Surrogate's Court considered that is just like a will. Just as what she said: Richard could not prove this will is under undue influence, involving perjury or forgery. The will drafter swore that Sydney was healthy enough to make a will.

Lawyer Woman in the Court

Okay. I understand the situation now. In America, our legal duty is to protect the decedent's benefit and respect their wishes. We will not make an exception for Richard Fishman. He has to take the responsibility for his behaviors. I will represent this court to reject this case. Richard will not get a hearing; his appeal is rejected.

Ext. Sydney's spirit

Haas is quoting the words I said when I altered my will ten years ago. Teresa asked for 50 percent of my assets, and I had to donate 50 percent to the college. I therefore had to put my family away with some excuses. After Teresa died, I mint to give all my money back to my family. I can't imagine that Curtain falsified that will and supported it with what I said ten years ago. He committed perjury in his affidavit on April 26, 2016. He was scared and withdrew that affidavit in the hearing day. Nobody noticed their trick, not even Pia at this moment.

Angel

Richard and Pia will have a long way to go. I don't know the ending of this case, as well.

Ext. In a subway station, Pia is pulling Richard out of the car before its door closes.

Pia

We are rejected by the Appellate Court, and we need to make the second appeal again. Let us find out the deadline first.

Ext. In the Appellate Court office.

Pia

We have spent so much time to prepare these books, the brief, and the backup document. Your clerk rejected us in twenty minutes. We can't even know what the judge said.

Clerk shows sympathy.

That is how it is. Today is the last day for you to make the second appeal in this court.

Pia

Thank you. We must appeal again. We meant to prepare this document in a Queens's library and submit that tomorrow. It is luck that we come here to find out the deadline first. We were in the train to Queens already. We stepped out of the train car at the last minute.

Clerk

It is good. You have to come before 5:00 p.m. today. Ext. In Seamon's office near the court room. A staff open the door for Pia, Richard.

Pia

Thank you. I believe Seamon must tell you that we need to use the computer in this office for a few hours.

Office Staff

Yes, you can use this one. If you have any problem, ask me.

Pia types what she wants to say in the brief first, and Richard helps her to correct the grammar mistakes. Ext. In the office of Appellate Division.

Pia

It is luck that my nephew's office is near here. We just prepared our document over there and come back in time.

Court Staff

Your second appeal is filed. Good luck, guys!

Ext. Sydney's spirit and the angel follow them all the time.

Sydney

I made Pia walk out of the subway car at the last moment. In the second appeal, she wrote down that Richard's mental problem messed up the family relationship. When answering Pia's brief, Palmer's lawyers dismissed even more documents. not just Curtain's affidavit, they dismissed things they submitted: doctor's note, the NJ court paper about Grandpa's visiting rights to Kenny's children and all Curtain's deposition.

Ext. Pia opens a letter from the court.

Voice from the Movie

Richard Fishman, your second appeal is rejected by this court, Appeal to Court to the New York of State.

Ext. Pia and Richard are in and out of the printing house. They serve summons and attach the affidavit with the court papers. They put things in a big box and mail that in the post office.

Pia

This is mailed to a courthouse in Albany. The deadline is two days after today. We pay for overnight service. Can you guarantee that this parcel can get there in time?

Post Office Clerk

It should have enough time. Let me check. What happened? The zip code you wrote down is not correct. This should be the right one. Do you want to change it?

Pia

Oh my god. I can't imagine the zip code was wrong when we send such important things before the deadline. Thank you very much. Do you always check the zip code for customers?

Post Office Clerk

Putting the correct zip code is your job, not ours. You are lucky that you have us to double check for you.

Ext. Sydney's spirit and the angel are around.

Sydney's spirit

Pia must wonder why every time the crucial mistakes she made were corrected at the last moment.

Angel

We try so hard to help them, and they are rejected again and again. Why do we keep they busy in this way? Is it some destiny related to this case?

Voice from the Movie

Without any explanation, Richard and Pia are rejected twice by the NY State Courts from Albany.

The screen shows **Appeal to the US Supreme Court**

Ext. Pia and Richard do research. Her computer shows: How can we appeal to the US Supreme Court."

A print house's name pops up. Pia sends an email. it spoke

We have to prepare some document for an appeal to the US Supreme Court. Please tell us, what do we need to do?

Ext. Pia's phone rings

Email Answer

Email us your brief and the backup document. We will tell you what to do.

The Other Side

We received your documents relate to your appeal to the US Supreme Court. They require things to be printed in a book size: 8.5 by 11 inches. It doesn't need to submit the original document to them because we have license to guarantee that everything in the book agrees with the original documents. The documents you provided now will be very expensive when make a book. I call you to explain the situation.

Pia

How much does it cost now?

Editor from the Print House

About eight thousand dollars, plus the filing fee will be over ten thousand dollars. You can cut it to five or six thousand dollars. We will charge by the pages you submit.

Pia

Thank you for your good service. We have spent one hundred thousand dollars for the legal fee and did short of funds. Are any pacific format does the Supreme Court require besides our points? We know nothing about that. Can you refer us to an expert and write what they need for us? We will pay for that.

Editor from the Print House

I read your case. You are robbing by a group of criminals. I will find some law students to complete the brief for you. You need petition for a writ of mandamus before your start mentioning your arguments.

Pia

Thank you very much.

Ext. Pia and editor on the phone.

After a while ...

Editor from the Print House

Hi. I received your final copy. Why does it miss the part we prepare for you? That is required by court!

Pia

Really? The final copy I approved doesn't include that part? I appreciate your help and didn't delete anything. Let me check.

Pia

Oh my god! The file I sent to you is the wrong file. If you did not follow it up, it would have caused big trouble for us. That file's page number is not agreeing with the page number we indicated in the brief. If I printed that, our appeal will be useless because the page numbers are not match.

Sydney's Spirit

I made people in the print house help her. All the errors she made are huge. She might realize that some power is blessing them.

The appeal to the Supreme Court must list four questions in summary and those questions must be able to impact the legal world.

Voice from the movie

Should we ignore a forgery initial just because our law does not require an initial in each page to make a will valid?

Should we allow lawyers conceal a person's psychiatric problem but accuse his crazy behaviors that cause him a big loss in an inheriting?

Should we ignore the docent's recorded statement instead of recognizing a will drafter's affirmation without any support by video or audio tape? When draft will for blind men, besides read the will aloud in front of witnesses, shouldn't video and audiotapes be mandatory required by law?

Angel

It is interesting that she will add her opinions about how to reduce government's debt in the brief. It is unusual but not breaking the law. Let us see what happen.

Chapter 13

PROPOSAL FOR DECREASING GOVERNMENT'S DEBT

Ext. In Pia's apartment, Pia and Richard

Pia

Richard, I am going to add some ideas in the brief that have nothing to do with this case. They are related to reducing government's debt. Do you mind if I discuss about that? Our case is insignificant compared with what I want to say. This is my only chance to reach the lawmakers in a high level.

Richard

You can say whatever you want to say and do whatever you want to do. I don't mind.

Voice from the Movie

Pia cares about world affairs all her life. Comparing with what she worries, the increasing of U.S. government's debt, Fishman's court case is not a big deal for her. She attaches her proposals in the brief and hopes can cause the law makers attention. Her basic ideas are stop provide free lunch, must make people work for what they need. She suggests to build up communities that have connection with manufactures and farms. For the free shelters, health care, food and transportation their people must work for $5/ hour and help our manufacture move back to the United States.

Socialist concepts about distribution and discipline should be applied to manage this world. Capitalist freedom and profit concept should be recognized as well.

To reduce the debt, we should stop providing free lunch, and give up capitalist consumption and competition. Instead, we should promote simple life, enrich people by providing them friendship and entertainment. Letting people live together in a community can meet our goal easily. We can rely on the cooperation's between the government, manufactures and civilization which have the same background, such as church, college, emigrants from the same country and clubs for sport fans.

Ext. Movie shows different size of Musk's box houses, studio, one bedroom, two bathrooms with windows. Prices are listed next to them. Outside of that there are public place for activity, TV room, poker room, room for dancing and room have piano for singing.

Movie screen show clinic where have AI doctors dealing with patients.

Words are typed in the screen: all facilities are pay by onetime payment but can be used for ten years or more. Huge rent is saved and Medicare expenses are under control in these kinds of facilities.

Ext. In classroom, College students are talking each other. Thinking about how to survive.

Student 1

I don't know what majored I should select now. It looks like all the good pay jobs, doctor or computer engineers will be substituted by AI eventually.

Student 2

We can't let Capitalist invisible hand to handle our future anymore. Its concept of consumption creates debts. Its competition cause conflicts between countries and make people jealous.

Student 3

The main points are after they alluring to spend the money, they create jobs in elsewhere. We have to study hard get into good school and have to struggle hard to please our bosses. Still, we might lose our job at our middle age and have mortgage waiting to pay. I feel sick about the situation they put us in. We have to make our own project and live in our own way. We will focus how to make a living but not memory those history events, scientist formulas. We can ask AI in case we need that.

Ext. Screen shows things students are doing: They contact government, applying for lands. They contact manufacturers that produce grocery.

Student 1

We can work for you for 5$/h if you can provide us free shelters and medical care.

Student 2

You can pay one payment to buy Musk's box house that average cost a few ten thousand dollars. You can let AI doctors to monitor our health. In long tern you can save big money from the salary you save. You actually are step into the real-estate and medical field with that kind of investment.

Student 3

We can sign contract and make sure we have good performance in the job even though we get only $5/h salary rate. We will help to manage the community, using friendship and entertainments to enrich our lives. We seek for simple life but no more high salary.

Boss of a manufacture

We move out of this country because it make us pay 20$/h here. If as what you suggest, paying 5$/h we can save $2400 per month. With that we can pay what you need, free shelter, Medicare, food, transportation and Wi-Fi. We can even cover your vacation once a year. Israel has some kind of farms run things in this way and they make profit meanwhile.

I can provide a lot more jobs if you can bring the salary rate down to $5/hr. You can get fund from government if you accept people who are taking welfare. One-time payment for Musk's box house and AI doctors can save huge money for government in long term.

Ext People from a same church, from the same alumni association, immigrants from the same country, sports fans from the same team and convince them to build their own projects or community by contacting with manufacturers.

They get the architectural graphics ready for their future house project. They convince the charity funds to give out donations or make financial investment directly.

They manage their facilities with their knowledge related to social work; design attractive forms of entertainment; host parties with dancing and singing; have basketball, baseball, or even poker contests between different communities. Such types of entertainment are the key point and selling point to the tenants.

Ext. In the morning, people go on the bus and just take ten minutes to get to their working area, either a factory or a farm.

Tenant 1 in the Bus

It is so convenient now. When I lived in NYC, I have to spend four hours a day on commute. I got $25 an hour, but after paying rent, utility, medical fee, transportation, and food, I have no savings. Now they cover everything. The $5 salary rate can give me $800 pocket money a month. I don't know; how can they work things out? Make everybody win.

Tenant 2 in the Bus

I think they save a lot of money, or you can say they make money on the housing and medical service they provide. Before we spend $2,000 on rent. They only spend a few ten thousand to build the apartments in one time. Assume that they s a v e $ 2 0 0 0 from the salary rate; it just takes a few years for them to have the investment back. In this way they are the landlord and their AI doctors involve heath care business as well. We become their potential customers.

They make money from rent to offset the salary they are supposed to pay us. The same principle makes government save huge medical expense. If not rely on AI doctors at least medical cost are under control by government's medical team.

Ext. At the farm, the sunshine is nice. A few tenants work near in some continents and a few of them work in a greenhouse next to it.

When windows in the continents are opened water comes out from there, Fish and shrimp are fell into a basket automatically.

People

Should we send the water to the greenhouse today?

People in the Greenhouse

Yes, the roots of the vegetables will clean up the fish's excretion in the water. We then put that back to the container to raise fish and shrimp again. To have such food we even don't need mud in land. It just needs a continent of water, food and set up temperature we can meat and vegetables we need.

Ext. Movie shows how the vegetable with long roots stretches to the water and is being fertilized by the fish's excretion. Vegetable growth very green and nice under the sunshine.

Technician in front of the Container

We have to make sure the inside environment is good for fish growth. Every few months, we can sell they in the market and make some income.

Ext. People send vegetables, fish, and shrimp to the kitchen. The chicken and pork raised in the farm are also ready there.

Worker from the Farm talk to the cook

Here is your organic food. It is your turn to make it delicious. What are you going to cook today?

Cook in the Kitchen

We are from Mexico. We will use Mexican way to cook it. Tomorrow is the Chinese on duty. You can vote and tell what kind of food you like the most. We will make what you like.

People Working in the Farm

Are you a good cooker?

Cooker

We like to cook, and we learn a lot here. Anybody can register in the kitchen instead of working in the factory, in the greenhouse, or in the farm.

Ext. People play basketball or baseball in the playground. There are tournaments among different communities. People can also have poker tournaments, not for money but for being the winners. People dance and sing at the party at night.

Voice from the movie

The tenants are existing workers, welfare collectors, and retired seniors. It actually helps the government step into the real estate field and medical fields, make profit to compensate society's needs, and triple their investment on the real estate field.

Pia Pikwah Fields

Ext. In an open square of a senior citizen home. A group of retired people is dancing and singing. A woman steps out when she hears a bell ring.

Woman (*tells her partner*)

I am on duty today; I have to go to see what the person needs. He is ringing the bell.

Ext. She walks in to a room where an old lady is lying on the bed.

The Old Lady

I need to go to the restroom. The woman helps the lady get up and walk into the bathroom.

The Old Lady

I am fine now. You can do whatever you want to do. If I need you, I can ring the bell again. I do need help but not every minute. Before, I had a lady sit in my home eight hours a day and get $200 pay from the government. Somepeopleclaim24-hourserviceandmakethegovernment pay $15,000 a month to them. All the money are disturbed by the family members. That is why we have so much deficit.

The Woman

I don't get paid and I work for the home care service that I might need in the future. Before walking into this room, I was dancing. Taking care of you in this way is easy for me. I am not qualifying to get free home care. Providing service here I don't need to worry anymore.

I like this place because the rent is cheap. I have an apartment in NY City that ate up my $250,000 and still needed me to pay over $1,000 maintenance a month. A place that has home care service will charge us $8,000 monthly for just a half room. Now I only pay $800 for a studio. I sold my apartment in NYC and have $250,000 as my pocket money plus the home care I have in the future.

Ext. Saturday and Sunday

There are sport competitions between different communities. There are cheerleading holding the must win slogan to follow with the athlete. The desire of wanting their baseball, basketball teams win is enough to drive the audiences crazy.

A few buses are waiting in the playground. Each bus has a sign for its destination. It has beach, downtown city, and casino. People get into the bus according to their earlier registration.

Ext. At the beach, tenants of the retirement home are walking together. Some take pictures. Ext. Tenant downtown.

Leader

You can go shopping or have lunch with your friends, but you have to come back here before three o'clock, and we will leave at four o'clock to go home.

Ext. In the retirement home, people stay around and are chatting.

Tenant 1

I bought a beautiful dress for my granddaughter yesterday in downtown. I hand it to her when we have tea in the afternoon. I am glad that we are still so close after I moved here.

Tenant 2

We live in the suburb but can enjoy life in New York City easily. I went to Central Park yesterday and listened to their free concert on the grass.

Tenant 3

Yesterday, I won $50 in the slot machine in the casino and left right away. My life has no big change since I moved into this retirement center, except I have more friends and more activities. Before, I traveled alone to the casino; if I lost money, I felt even more lonely. However, I can't help but to go there because I had no company and had nothing to do at home. I can't imagine how to spend my day if I am old and cannot walk around anymore.

Tenant 4

I have the same worry. Thing's seniors' need the most are health and company. When I stay home, I have no energy to watch TV or go out every day. I sit on the sofa, waiting for the night. I then wait for the sun to rise. Now, even though I can't sing or dance, I can sit on the wheelchair and share you guys' happiness. It is good that this place has people from different ages. They make me feel young.

Voice from the Movie

Pia's proposal is also designed for emigrants who need shelters and jobs. We directly produce from green resources. It doesn't need to fight for jobs in the market.

Ext. Emigrants are sent to the farms that use containers and greenhouses to produce ingredients.

Emigrant 1

There are too many gangs in our country. Some of them kidnap the children. Theyoncecuta child'shandbecausehis parents could not pay. We just need a piece of land to settle down. We don't mind the life is simple, as long as it is stabilized and secure. A small peaceful land and ways to survive is what I am looking for.

Emigrant 2

I was misled by the capitalist concepts about making more money and maximizing consumption. I travel so far from my country and suffer so much. Now I realize that it not worth it. If things are organized like this, I don't mind to stay in my hometown instead of running around.

Voice in the Movie

Capitalist consumption misled us to spend more money than we make. Its competitions create angry losers who are waiting for free lunch from our government. That is why our debt keeps going up. We have no reason to believe such system is the best system and provoke wars to defend it. We should try to use both capitalist and socialist system to manage our world, to fight against poverty and eliminate war. Just eliminate wars can save big money for our government.

Ext. Sydney Fishman's spirit and the angel

Sydney's Spirit

You know, her idea is similar to the kibbutzim farms in Israel. They use this way to settle the Jews emigrants from all over the world. People can choose to leave there. Rent, food is free there. Lawyer and custodians get the same pay that are low. I once suggested to Richard to move there. His mother thought I am going to send him to the war, and because of that, he hated me more.

Angel

I know what you mean. Pia has that idea because she grew up in China, a socialist country without concept of consumption and competition. Now she promotes it not through dictatorship or street riots but by changing the new generation approaching.

Sydney's Spirit

The Chinese own a lot of debt, after adopt Capitalist consumption and commutation concept. The whole world cannot stand their comparative prices as well. We do need to reevaluate everything.

Angle

Competition make life much more difficult: People must study hard for getting into a good school; must find a good job with high pay; must please their bosses to maintain their jobs. They might lose their jobs at their forties when mortgage and credit cards are waiting to be paid. The Chinese new generation already realize such endings. They stop to consume, get marry, buy houses and have children. They live in a very simple way, lying flat

Sydney's Spirit

I know now. We make Pia go so far because only the Supreme Court requires, they submitted their brief in the size of 8.5 by 11. That makes her think of publishing the case as a book and promotes her period book, as well

Angel

We will see. She is not a hardworking person, but she is intelligent and sensitive. She might realize that a power is blessing them.

Chapter 14
POSTSCRIPT

The movie screen shows big words: "This case is filed in New York State Commission on Judicial Conduct."

Ext.Pia and Richard stand in front of a building in downtown Manhattan, 61 Broadway. Convict 19 just start to spread. People work at home instead of go to office for avoiding catch virus. Inside the closed building they have someone received mails for the offices.

Pia

They said if a judge does not let you talk or ignores what you say, by federal law, you have the right to complain. The commission has eleven members to read the case. It looks like they are more serious than the court clerk. However, they don't care about the consequence of the court decision. That means they might punish the judge; they don't fix the error the judge made. We will have no way to get your father's money back.

Richard

It is correct; anybody has the right to complain about judge's conduct.

Sydney's Spirit

All my money was stolen by those bitches? I believe that; those are still my money and I will spend it as Lewis's son. Right now, I prevent Lewis's contact with any woman until they win the case. If I become Pia's grandson I will fulfill Pia's dream, build up kibbutzim. Over there, I provide free shelters, food, medical service, and jobs. I will do something for the society and make profit for myself, as well.

Angel

Your wish is interesting. Let us see what happens. We also let Pia complain to the Attorney Grievance Committee. They rejected her complaint about Haas but accepted her complain to Curtain. It looks like they are investigating the will-drafter, Curtain. He was the only one who made the sworn and deposition but then withdrew them. That obvious was involving perjuries and is considered committing crime.

We make her publish two books and make this case to an ongoing story.

The screen shows the copy of a book, "*An Appeal to the US Supreme Court and a Proposal to Our President*" and then another book" A Ten Million $ Testament"

Voice from the movie

Pia starts to believe justice might never come. In our bureaucracy system, lawmakers tend to defend each other, care about their dignity more than care about the dignity of laws. They get pay but prefer to do nothing and change nothing. Below is what happening after all the appeals were failed. She worries about Richard's situation but feels very helpless.

Ext. Pia on phone with staff from Richard's facility.

Staff

Hi, is Richard stay in your apartment overnight? We didn't see him here.

Pia

No, he left last night at about seven PM.

Staff

OK. We have call 911, because he is like a child who doesn't know what he is doing sometime.

Ext. Policemen knock Pia's apartment

Ext. Pia on phone

Policemen

Is Richard still in your apartment?

Pia

No. Thank you for your concern, please let me know when you have news about him.

Pia

Richard where were you last night. The phone number shows you are back to your facility now.

Richard

Yes, I am fine now. I lost my way and could not find the subway station until this morning. I hang out in the street all night.

Pia

You were in and out of Flushing's subway for a hundred times. How come you lost your way. It is luck that I gave you a Jacket before you walked away my apartment.

Ext. In a bus station at night Richard and Pia

Pia

The bus will come in a few minutes. I will send you to the subway station. Richard, you have come see me in the morning. In that way you have enough to go home and don't get lost.

Richard didn't say anything. All of a certain he yells to the other customers who waiting in the bus station.

Richard

You are all criminals. I want to kill you! I want to kill you!

Richard runs away quickly and left the bus station. Pia run after him.

Pia

Richard, don't go that direction, you will lose you way and hang out in the street again.

Richard didn't stop and kept going. Pia ran after him and didn't give up. Richard is on the direction to the subway even though he didn't know. Pia was over seventy years old. it is not easy to follow Richard who walk very fast. It is luck that there is moon that night. Pia gazing the moon, take a big breath and continue running after Richard. She must make sure Richard get into the subway otherwise he will stay in the street again.

Pia

Go that way, the Subway station is over that side.

Richard stops for a while and go toward to the direction Pia points.

Richard yell to the sky again.

You are criminals; you stole my money.

> Pedestrians are scared and walk away from him. When close to the subway, Richard walked into a building and from the other side of the glass door he pitches to Pia. He is angry to everybody and he looks dangers.

Pia pulls him out of that building.

Pia

This is a lobby of a motel. You can't get in or they will call policemen.

Ext. Finally they reach the subway station, Pia pays the subway fare for Richard and give him forty dollars.

Ext. In Pia's apartment. Richard is eating and then take a lap in the Sofa.

Pia

It has been four years after we lost the case. Richard it is good that you called me every week for an appointment. I don't mind to give you money in case you need it. I just want to make sure you are OK.

Richard has no reaction on his face

Pia

Let me cut you beard before you go home. If you don't smell like that, I can take you to the barber shop.

She uses a scissors to cut Richard's beard little by little. She doesn't know how to use a plane, and Richard doesn't trust her to use the plane as well.

Richard is standing there and still has no expression in his face.

When finishing cutting the beard, Pia gives Richard a clean T shirt and tell him to change it.

Pia

You must look clean and not smell, otherwise you will be discriminated in the subway train.

Richard picks up the food Pia prepare for him and walk away without say anything.

Pia

Let us keep touch, Richard. I want to hear from you and make sure you are OK. Every time I call you, I get no answer from the phone.

Richard

They just make the transfer but the phone in my room not working at all.

Richard walks away and close the door behind him. Ext Pia and Richard are on phone.

Richard

I decide not see you and Lewis again. Lewis hit me many years ago and he might do the something again. I cut your hand, you might seek revenge and hurt me one day...

Richard hangs up the phone and he really never calls Pia again.

Ext Richard facing close to a piece of wall for and not moving. People passing by are kicking him. He spit and shout at them. People complain to the social worker.

Social Worker

Richard, you have to behave yourself or we will bring you to court and kick you out of this facility.

Ext In the Court room

Lawyer of the facility

Richard was very crazy. He refuses to take medicine because he doesn't think he is schizophrenia. We need a court order to keep him in the hospital or we must to kick him out.

Lens get close to Richard. There is miserable expression in his face and he says nothing.

Voice from the movie

Pia shows up in the court try to tell people that Richard actually was autistic in the very beginning. She is very helpless and hopeless for the situation that they encounter. However, she still spent another fifty thousand dollars to republish and promote her books with all the proposals. She hopes when we cannot reform a bureaucracy system, we can try to build up our own world and have life we want there.

In her proposal, for the $5/h salary rate people don't have to pay tax. They don't pay for the social security system as well and they plan to home care each other when get old. They believe social security system actually is a Ponzi Scheme that gives people nothing eventually. They get rid of the control from a bureaucratic government and let it find money to corrupt and waste on its own.

For building up the new world, we don't rely on street riot but by changing young generation's approaching. We just need a piece of land where there are no wars, no gangs, and no competition. We produce ingredients and groceries that we need. We do not seek for high salaries, but rely on friendship and entertainment to enrich our life. Our lives will be simple and happy.

Pia hopes our new generation are happy. She herself is unable to sense happiness anymore for she once witnessed the tragic experiences that happened in Fishman's family.

Pia Fields
Finish in Flushing New York At July 4th 2025

www.ingramcontent.com/pod-product-compliance
Lightning Source LLC
Chambersburg PA
CBHW020458030426
42337CB00011B/153